Sally Magnusson was born an[d ...] After starting as a reporter on the *Scotsman*, she moved to London and television journalism, presenting BBC's Breakfast News among other programmes. Since her return to Scotland, she has anchored the BBC's Reporting Scotland, and is a frequent presenter of Songs of Praise.

FAMILY LIFE

Sally Magnusson

HarperCollins*Publishers*

Many of these stories first appeared in the *Herald*.
Some have been revised and expanded
for their publication in book form.

HarperCollins*Publishers*
77–85 Fulham Palace Road,
Hammersmith, London W6 8JB

www.**fire**and**water**.com

This paperback edition 2000
1 3 5 7 9 8 6 4 2

First published in Great Britain
by HarperCollins*Publishers* 1999

Copyright © Sally Magnusson 1995, 1996, 1997, 1998, 1999

The Author asserts the moral right to
be identified as the author of this work

ISBN 0 00 653124 5

Set in Bembo by
Rowland Phototypesetting Limited, Bury St Edmunds, Suffolk

Printed and bound in Great Britain by
Caledonian International Book Manufacturing Ltd, Glasgow

For Jamie, Siggy, Anna Lisa, Rossie,
Magnus and Norman

Acknowledgements

My thanks to Anne Johnstone for encouraging me to write, Jackie McGlone for her unstinting support at the *Herald*, Susan Watt of HarperCollins for her enthusiasm, and most of all my family for allowing me to plunder their lives for copy – my sons, daughter, mother, father, aunt Anna, sisters Topsy and Margaret, brother Jon and long-suffering husband Norman, who says the royalties had better be worth it.

Contents

INTRODUCTION

Exodus

The matter under discussion that night, at the end of a balmy evening in the late summer of 1994, was really very simple. Where on earth would we put a fifth child?

The Buckinghamshire cottage that had seemed so palatial when we moved in with one small son was under strain. We now had four children neatly stacked in two bedrooms the size of a couple of horse-boxes. There was an au pair in the room up the back stairs and a visitor on the living-room floor with his feet nearly up the chimney. Our own room, a centuries-old hayloft where sheep-traders once slept on their way to the Thames, was big on romantic features like low black beams, bulging walls and curvy windows that opened straight into the arms of a lilac tree, but so short on space that our bed more or less filled it.

We were sitting on this now. Or at least my husband was sitting on it; I was lying flat out in that attitude of luxurious release that comes with the delivery of the last story and the last drink and the last dummy to the last child in a bedtime process that has taken the last three hours. My partner, I recall, had a pen and paper in his hand, presumably to lend a businesslike air to our deliberations, although I don't remember him actually writing anything.

The question we were applying our minds to that night was, in point of fact, a hypothetical one. There was no fifth child on the way. But for some months now there had been a sort of feeling in the air that a fifth child might well find itself on the way if we

3

didn't come up with a few good reasons why it shouldn't. The time to remind ourselves of these had come.

This was a radical departure from normal procedure. Numbers one to four had made it to this world without so much as a second's sensible planning and for regrettably frivolous reasons like my fancying a spot of maternity leave, or reading an article about a sure-fire, foolproof way to make daughters (it wasn't), or getting carried away by a heady sensation of well-being and daring induced by the novelty of not having yawned once that day. But by the time we began to flirt with the notion yet again, there being something so pleasing (as my husband said) about the number five, the reasons for not doing it were beginning to pile up so high that even the rashest of romantics, the most reckless of begetters, had to take note.

For a start, that ticklish question: where would we put a fifth child? We did a quick mental tour of the house. 'There's always the bathroom,' my husband concluded weakly. 'It's very warm in there.' Where exactly in the bathroom? 'Er, the bath. We could fit a carry-cot in there.' Under close questioning he was forced to concede that babies didn't remain in carry-cots very long and graduating to a bed in the airing cupboard held few attractions. Anyway, where would we put the towels?

No, there was nothing else for it. If we had another baby, we would have to move. From this point, there was no stopping the momentum of the anti-baby case. I'd have to stop work again, and how would we afford a bigger mortgage for a bigger house if I couldn't help pay for it? And we'd need a bus to drive around in. And no one would invite us anywhere – it was bad enough with four. And being pregnant made me sick. And we'd had barely a night's sleep in nine years. And it would mean another two years of nappies. And I'd be one of those ancient mothers at the school gate that everyone thinks is a granny. And, heaven help us, it might be twins.

It did all seem rather clear-cut when you looked at it that way. But my husband, still trying to be businesslike, said we ought to look at the other side of the balance-sheet. Positive benefits of further child.

4

There was a longish pause. I said something about it being lovely for the daughter to have a sister, it just not being the same for a girl with brothers.

'And if it's a boy?'

Well, we'd love him, of course. And I'd always be able to tell the daughter we'd done our best on the sister front. Anyway, there was this article I'd been reading, this *different* article . . .

The case, we could both see, was weak. 'Is that it?' he asked.

Well, yes, that *was* it. How could I even begin to put into words this feeling, this small feeling, this daft, irrational, ridiculous, very strong feeling that there was someone else who simply needed to be born?

'So to summarize,' said he, 'we have a list of extremely good reasons considerably longer than your arm for not adding any more children to this family, including' (he looked meaningfully around his beloved hayloft) 'moving away from this house. And we have no reason whatsoever for doing it except that, despite our dismal track record in the conception of sisters, we think it's nice to have them. Is that a fair summary of the position?'

It was.

'So are we going to go for it?'

We grinned at each other. Of course we were.

A few months into the pregnancy I took the daughter aside and explained that I was very sorry but she wasn't going to have a sister. This information came courtesy of a kindly ultrasound operator at the maternity hospital who had said she would have a look on the scan for me so that I could deal with all those people who insisted on saying, 'Oh, you're pregnant again. You must be hoping it's a girl.'

She warned me that there was a fifty per cent chance of getting it wrong. 'Even at this stage,' she was saying as she zoomed over my abdomen with a thing like a computer mouse dipped in hair gel, 'you can never be quite sure of the sex and . . .' The mouse stopped dead in its tracks. 'Oh, my goodness me,' she said breathlessly, 'well I never, there's no mistake about that.'

We both peered at the screen. The appendage in question was, she assured me, a whopper, and I could forget the fifty per cent margin of error. This was pure boy.

The daughter, who had greeted the birth of a male cousin some two years previously with the grumpy observation that there were 'too much boys in this family', was aghast. But the ultrasound photograph with its conclusive evidence of manhood proved so diverting that she was soon junking the polished shell that she had planned to display to the Reception class at 'show and tell' the next day in its favour. After this triumphant piece of one-upmanship, her devotion to the fourth brother never wavered.

Finding a house was more of a problem. At the time we were happily positioned just far enough from London to see a field now and then but not so far distant as to require you to take a packed lunch for the journey to work down the M40. A cursory glance at the property pages revealed that a house with the sort of dimensions that would keep the baby out of the bath and guests out of the chimney, with enough character to satisfy the romantic soul of the head of the family and a price roughly equal to what we'd get for our cottage, would take us so far outside London that, frankly, we might as well go and live in Scotland.

So we did.

In April 1995 we headed north. Half the street turned out to wave goodbye as the new eight-seater van trundled off up the road towards the M40, groaning with boxes, bags, children, rabbit, au pair and thirty-six weeks worth of pregnant wife. My husband said he felt like Moses. I think the neighbours thought we were bonkers.

The reasons for moving such a distance away had proved a little hard to explain. It was about so many things. The lure of green hills. The yen to be in on what looked increasingly likely to be the birth of a Parliament in my homeland. Wanting to be closer to the extended family, a desire not wholly unconnected with the baby-sitting facilities on offer although I'd like to assure my mother that these were not the only reason. Lower house prices. The electronic revolution that meant offices could be just about anywhere. Aeroplanes that got you from Glasgow to Heathrow faster than you could cover a couple of miles of London's Westway on a wet Friday.

So many reasons and none of them the real one, or at least the most compelling one. Between ourselves we knew the real reason was love.

My husband likes a house with a bit of character and romance. In fact he loves that sort of place with a passion that those of us who think a few bricks slung together in roughly the right proportions are all that's required may find hard to understand. But he grew up in Hartlepool, on England's industrial north-east coast, which probably explains everything. Even its most defiant admirers would concede that Hartlepool is a bit low on romantic housing stock.

So nothing, not even, I suspect, the imminent arrival of sextuplets, would have induced this man to leave his cottage with the bendy walls and the sheep-traders' hayloft if he had not experienced that same *coup de foudre* for somewhere else. But on a Christmas visit to Scotland the previous December, on one of those dark, dreary, drizzly afternoons when nothing is looking its best, least of all a house in the wilds that has lain empty for months, it happened. He came, he saw, he fell for it. Neither a half-mile hike to the house next door nor a surveyor's report to strike terror into any sensible purchaser's heart would deter him. From that moment, we were on our way.

The trouble was that, being strong on soul but weaker on more prosaic details like a rain-proof roof and rot-free walls, the house was not actually in a position to accommodate us when we bought it, which meant that my parents and the aunt who lives with them found themselves seeing considerably more of us than they had expected.

It's not everyone who would welcome the children of Israel (plus rabbit) into their home without any clear idea of when the Promised Land would be ready for occupation, but when the big green van trundled up to their front door that April evening and disgorged us one by one, they gave every impression of being pleased to see us. They supplied all the comforts of home for weeks on end, only drawing the line eventually at the rabbit, who developed an uncomfortable relationship with their Labrador and was dispatched to live with the workmen at the new house.

I, meanwhile, grew ever vaster, so much so that my aunt began to have palpitations every time I left the house, convinced that no one could reach that size without bursting, or at the very least giving urgent birth in the middle of Tesco's. We had hoped to be in the new homestead before either of these scenarios developed, but then we've always been a bit innocent about builders. In the race between the dry rot and the baby, there was no contest.

He started arrival proceedings one evening in the middle of the film *Rob Roy*, which I reckoned was a fitting omen for the one child in the family whom I might be able to count on to cheer for the right side at Murrayfield. I had begun to suspect things were on the move when I found I couldn't make it up Glasgow's Renfield Street without clinging to every second lamp-post and counting slowly to twenty. While prising me away from the last lamp-post, my husband did mention that maybe it wasn't a cinema we should be heading for. But with the sang-froid of childbirth veterans, we went and bought the tickets anyway. We knew this was going to be our last night on the town before succumbing to round-the-clock milking and the kind of fatigue that has you dozing off in the middle of the adverts for Häagen-Dazs and Gordon's gin. We were not about to surrender it.

So as the claymores clashed and the corpses rolled, I sat surreptitiously timing contractions. The prospective father, taking nonchalance just a degree too far, I felt, passed over his watch and asked if I was sure I couldn't manage some popcorn. We stayed to the bloody end, even hanging around with some bravado to see if we knew anybody on the credits, and then drove straight to the maternity hospital, where number five duly joined us.

A few weeks afterwards we all finally moved into the new house. The children announced, to a man, that they didn't like it and wanted to go back to the old one. The eldest added that he hated Scotland and would be leaving home at the earliest opportunity to return to England. How old exactly did you have to be to leave home? The daughter said she thought she could get used to it if she could only have a dog; they had been promised a dog if we ever lived on a quiet road and you couldn't get a much quieter road than this one since we were the only people on it, so when would the puppy be arriving?

The clamour for a dog showed no sign of abating. Chief among the persuaders was their father, who proved impervious to the argument, my argument, that to add a puppy to this chaos of children, painters, joiners, unopened tea chests, newborn baby and homesick rabbit was even by our standards an act of madness. He wanted a Gordon setter, the Scottish version of the Irish setter, which he reckoned would be good with children while at the same time, owing to its black and tan colouring, stood every chance of being mistaken by any aspiring burglar for a Rottweiler. As my mother observed tartly, a blind man running for a bus wouldn't notice the difference.

Still, I have only myself to blame, because I was the one in the end who spotted the fateful advert in the paper for a litter of Gordon setter puppies and was daft enough to mention it to the assembled company. They were in the car and off to collect one before you could say Life Will Never Be The Same Again.

And it wasn't. The second incontinent newborn to join the household proved to be a lovable basket case, as gentle, beautiful and comprehensively loopy as the rest of the breed. More so, probably, because we were all too busy to train her and she developed a taste for doing exactly what she liked from an early age. Her favourite pastime was to hurtle round the house overturning waste-paper bins and scrabbling through the contents in search of tissues, an enduring fetish that explains why to this day the carpets of every bedroom are so prettily festooned with white confetti.

It was not long after this that a friend with whom I had worked many years before on a Sunday newspaper came to visit. I think it was the day the pizza burned while I was mopping up dog poo. 'You should write about this, you know,' she said. 'Give us all a laugh.' A few days later I had the features editor of her paper, the Glasgow-based *Herald*, on the phone asking when I could start.

For the next two or three years I wrote a column about whatever was going on that week on the home front. It was a period when our family life encompassed not only children, mad animals, visitors, au pairs and, at one time, a lodger, but also had to accommodate my husband's erratic schedule as a drama director and my own resumed presenting work on the BBC's *Breakfast News*. The programme had put up graciously with my many maternity-inspired absences over the years and welcomed me back even after our move to the opposite end of the country meant that I could only manage two days a fortnight. On those two days my husband exhausted himself in New Man mode at home and I regained my sanity in London.

This darting back and forwards between Glasgow and London every couple of weeks, while the children basked at home under the indulgent eye of their father, was really rather pleasant. I stayed at my sister's house in Hammersmith, revelling in the clatter of small children who were not my responsibility. Even being woken by infant wails at 2 a.m. when I had to be up an hour later for work produced nothing but mellow sympathy. I would merely turn over in my child-free bed and slip deliciously back to sleep.

This happy arrangement continued until my husband's own absences from home meant that I had to give up the commuting to London. It was all change again on the work front. Just as well that my strategy for motherhood and career has always been pretty fluid. I've adapted from baby to baby, adamant that I didn't have all these children merely to hand them over to someone else, but as ready as the next woman to escape in the right circumstances.

This, I suspect, is a more widespread attitude among mothers these days than you might think from the polarized rhetoric of some parenting gurus, who conspire to leave the impression that the choice is either staying at home or being a managing director. They all rather miss the point that many of us muddle along more or less happily somewhere in the middle. We may not be doing quite the job we could have tackled in child-free circumstances, but neither, thanks to dishwashers, supermarkets and men who no longer blush to change a nappy or rustle up the tea, is our mothering style quite what our own mothers' used to be.

We know that there are ways of working and amounts of time you can devote to it and people you can get to help you do it, which will have no adverse impact on the children. They will thrive, and so, with any luck, will you. We also know that you can overdo it. You can get the balance wrong, do too much, be away too often, get too stressed and end up being neither a useful employee nor a good mother. So you adjust. And motherhood seems to me quintessentially about adjusting: to circumstance, to need, to everyone else's convenience, to the new demands and new freedoms that come as children grow up, and above all to the dawning realization that, wherever you go and whatever you do in this life, these creatures you have spawned will be in your hair and coiled around your heart for ever.

It may be that the truth about a lot of modern mothering is in fact rather humdrum and resistant to sloganeering. I reckon that rather than wanting to 'have it all', many mothers at my stage of the family cycle are simply trying to have a bit more of some things like whinge-free conversation and privacy in the loo, and a bit less of others like cooking, chauffeuring, peace-keeping, clothes-washing, nose-wiping and bottom-cleaning. If someone is kind enough to pay us for this small adjustment, so much the better.

Being a freelance means that I've been able to vary my working life more easily than most. When I was still in England looking after three children under five, I did very little else, although I do remember once spending several days presenting a live wildlife series called *Badgerwatch* from a bizarre woodland studio somewhere on the south coast, while my mother (lured from her northern redoubt by the offer of a balmy holiday by the sea) trudged endlessly up and down the windy promenade with a fractious four-month-old grand-daughter. My husband had the toddler and the four-year-old to himself at home. Despite spending the evenings waiting for a badger to snuffle into view and half the night trying to express enough breast-milk to last the daughter through the next day, I found the experience exhilarating and perversely restful, although I think it's fair to say the other two didn't.

I did go down with pneumonia a few days later, mind you, and it was then that my mother started lobbying for us to get some help. So we squeezed into the already bulging cottage a flame-haired temptress from New Zealand, first in an heroic line of au pairs, who eventually enabled me to make one of my periodic returns to breakfast television for part of the week. They came fast and furious after that. To date, following the departure of the New Zealander to pursue a racier life in the capital, we've had one girl from Norway, two from Holland, two from Iceland, two from the Czech Republic and one all the way from High Wycombe. No one can say we haven't done our bit for international relations.

At the time of our great exodus to the north we had with us a formidably efficient Dutch au pair called Nezia, who was delighted to take over the business of opening tea-chests and finding places for everything while I settled the older children into school and stuffed cabbage leaves down my nursing bra to combat the agonies of mastitis. Come to think of it, it was two years before I got round to putting the plates where I actually wanted them in the kitchen.

Loud and large-hearted, Nezia was the great boon of our early days in Scotland. Her duties ranged from removing the puppy a dozen times a day from the waste-paper bins to travelling round the Hebrides with me on a *Breakfast News* special, keeping number five baby amused between feeds. Before long she was practically running the household and I was delighted when she confessed one day to an overwhelming passion for the postman. I had high hopes of her settling down here and organizing our lives for ever. Unfortunately the postman gave no sign of noticing this seductress who raced to the door each day with cherry-glossed lips, proffering a pair of trembling hands for the mail. She returned home a year later and promptly got engaged to a Dutchman.

But it is to Nezia that I owe the few hours of peace I managed to snatch that year to start chronicling the ups and downs of our family life. It was a bonus to discover that writing the columns went a long way towards helping me retain a sense of humour and balance during that memorable period when I was the mother of five children under ten. I suppose it felt like a kind of victory to be able to impose some slight artistic order on the havoc by giving it a beginning, middle and end. On the day the dog ate the gerbil, the column was half written in my head before I had finished mopping up the entrails.

In hindsight I realize that the period covered by these pieces represents a particular flavour in my life which I am unlikely to taste again. ('You'd better believe it', I hear my husband bellowing.) It was a time filled with the unique sounds and softnesses of babyhood, shot through with the alternating euphoria and gloom that the tyranny of the infant bestows. It was also the period before we hit exams, adolescence and girlfriends at the other end of the family, when the relatively uncomplicated rhythms of primary school life held sway, with Hallowe'en costumes and nativity plays, sports days and summer fairs. By the end of it, the youngest was ready to launch himself on an unsuspecting world of playgroups and nurseries, and the eldest was eyeing up the vital statistics of the Spice Girls.

What had not changed, mind you, was the air of mild chaos about the place. A friend who works a lot with us was asked once by a sceptical aunt of hers if life in our house was really as it appeared in the columns. 'It is,' came the heartfelt reply. 'Believe me, it really is.'

But although these pieces, which open in October 1995, reflect my own particular brand of domestic disorder and crisis management, I hope they are not that far from the experience of other families, large and small, who live and love and laugh and cry together as we do, and who, for all the strains, are happy to be part of a uniquely precious institution.

At the same time I know that life for many families is something far removed from the cheerful trivia chronicled here. It is painful beyond the imaginings of those of us who talk blithely about ups and downs as if the dishwasher going on the blink mattered in the scheme of things, as if anyone who hasn't had to nurse a handicapped child twenty-four hours a day understands for one second

13

what real tiredness is, as if any gripe about parenthood is worth tuppence when all that counts is the simple privilege of having a child to cherish and hold close.

Go to a hospice for terminally ill children and you will see the triumph of family life over real stress and genuine hardship. You will see parents who survive the unimaginable, summoning reserves of fortitude and stoicism that shame the rest of us with our very small woes. They are the people I salute. Theirs is the family life, hewn from the hardest rock and the most unpromising circumstances, that I admire beyond any.

PART ONE

Milky Heaven

Last night we slept. All night. In the same bed from beginning to end. Ten and a half hours of deep, deep uninvaded slumber. It was delicious.

No wailing baby; no howling dog; no insomniac four-year-old bursting in with the urgent news that he's had a wonderful dream; none of the communal singing at dawn in which child number four is wont to lead the assembled bed in a rousing rendition of 'Old MacDonald Had a Farm', a point at which I usually slink off to feed four-month-old number five and my husband, rightly suspicious that I intend to find an empty bunk and steal some of the sleep that he's patently not going to get, demands to know where I think I'm off to.

Ah no. Last night we slept. We left the combined forces of mother, aunt, au pair and a brace of sisters to hold the fort in shifts and we escaped for twenty-four hours of solitude.

Goodness knows, we were ready for it. After what I calculate to be some 3,600 nights of floor-pacing and back-thumping, dummy-replacing and bed-hopping, marital camaraderie in the wee hours has been showing signs of strain.

These days it stretches about as far as the night's third wake. That's the point at which we both pretend to be asleep and not to have heard the baby who, as we both know, will wake at least two of the others if not silenced immediately.

Actually, to my intense chagrin, I've discovered lately that my husband is no longer pretending. These are real snores, dammit. I'm now faced with the dilemma of either waking him and feeling guilty because, as he's the first to point out, I'm awake anyway, or of letting him slumber on and doing the needful myself, again. The trouble is, in this sleep-hungry state one's finer instincts are a mite repressed. The soaring resentment of my being awake while he luxuriates noisily in the one commodity on earth I would kill for right now is – I'm ashamed to say – overpowering.

So much so that the other night, sitting up in bed in the darkness beside this snoring heap, hunched miserably over a colicky baby whose back it was his turn to rub, I thought I would just give him a little tap with my foot to alert him to the fact that I had generously taken on his watch.

Since number three had at some point in the night inserted herself between us, I had to stretch my leg a bit to reach across her with my little tap. And, OK, I admit it, I did rather misjudge the distance and the force required to bridge it.

A thunderous roar erupted from the other side of the bed. 'Did you kick me?' The bed-clothes rose like a wrathful Neptune from the deep. 'I don't believe it. DID YOU JUST KICK ME?'

I then had to listen, suitably shamed, to a lecture about what things had come to when a chap couldn't feel safe in his own bed. The dignity of this tirade was weakened somewhat by the revelation that the dream from which he had been so untimely ripped had ended abruptly with the comedian Jim Broadbent shooting him in the leg with a double-barrelled telescope.

Collapse of combatants in giggles. In all the excitement the baby fell asleep. And in the morning we decided we needed a break.

So here we are, enjoying our twenty-four hours in one of these hotels where they do things right. I'm still in bed, propped up against the soft, fat pillows in which I sank to oblivion last night. The remains of the largest breakfast I've ever eaten are on my lap, a cup of exquisite coffee steams within casual reach of my right hand, a fire is flickering in the grate and through the open window ahead of me a forest of red and yellow leaves is stirring faintly.

In a moment I will saunter through to the en-suite and immerse myself in a foaming white bath, without stubbing my toe on a toy soldier or running out of hot water because everyone's been in before me. Bliss. When you're savouring every minute, a twenty-four-hour break can feel like a fortnight's holiday.

There has only been one minor hitch. The reason we are awake at all right now and not clinging to sleep until we're turfed out, sobbing, is because of a little problem with milk. While the baby is at home downing the powdered stuff by the pint-load, his usual sources of nourishment don't know what's hit them, or rather what hasn't hit them. I woke up maddeningly early with two gigantic rocks clamped to my chest.

As all breast-feeding mothers know, the one fleeting compensation for all the physical indignities that childbirth brings upon you is that for a few months you have a figure worth several thousand pounds of surgery – from the waist up, anyway.

Unfortunately, like the bad fairy at the christening of the baby princess, Nature sweeps in to add one little proviso: 'Yes, you shall have wondrous breasts. They will be luscious and awe-inspiring. Men will drool at the sight of them. However, I will personally see to it that the bigger they are, the more they will hurt, the more they will leak and the less chance your rapturous partner will have of getting within a foot of them.'

Urgent deflation was required before I popped, so for half an hour I sat squirting milk into the hotel's best bath-towels, which must be about the least erotic thing you can do with a pair of breasts. My beloved gave up and went for a bath.

I think it's time to go home.

October, 1995

Mid-term Madness

All I can say is, it seemed a good idea at the time. Wiser heads might have deemed it inadvisable, if not downright reckless, even to contemplate a two-day holiday in a caravan, in October, in the rain, in a spot so far-flung that the journey itself took half the available time, with a gaggle of ailing children.

But on that dreich afternoon, with the children wondering dolefully why it was that everybody, absolutely *everybody* in their class would be going away somewhere and they were *always* stuck at home, I found myself impulsively ringing up a caravan park in deepest Argyllshire and booking us in the next day.

I washed clothes until midnight, arranged a complicated dog-feeding and key-hiding routine with my mother, restrained the children's attempts to pack their entire worldly goods and, more ominously, administered Calpol to the eldest, who was looking a bit flushed. For the first time, a little bubble of doubt broke the surface of my enthusiasm. I ignored it.

The next morning two things became clear. One was that you need as much gear for a two-day expedition with five children as you do for a month, and possibly a year. The second was that the eldest was ill, probably with the same throat infection for which number four was currently working his way through a bottle of penicillin. Off he went to the doctor, while I continued to assemble enough supplies for an assault on K2.

I packed: two bags of bed-linen, one bag of towels, two bags of rainwear, one bag of Wellingtons, one large bag with clothes for four children, one small bag with clothes for two grown-ups, one enormous bag with clothes for one baby plus nappies, wet-wipes, nappy-sacs and bottom cream, one travel cot, one buggy, one baby-walker, one bag of assorted rattles, one bottle-sterilizer, a selection of toys, *Beano* annuals, cuddly animals and cash-boxes, one bag of games, one box of food, one box of baby-food along with baby-milk, baby-plates and baby-spoons, one box of medicines including penicillin, Calpol, Calpol Six-Plus, gripe water, eczema cream and asthma inhalers, one nebulizer in case of asthma emergency, two packets of tissues, a bumper bag of crisps and one book for me.

This little lot was awaiting my husband when he and number one returned from the doctor's armed with yet another prescription for Erythroped.

'We can't possibly need all that stuff,' he groaned. I challenged him to remove anything we could conceivably do without, bearing in mind that it had started to rain and would probably do so for the next two days.

'Right, I will.' He strode to the teetering pile, cast a keen eye over it, barked a few questions about contents, and finally removed the baby-walker. He then added – added, mark you – some reading material of his own (oh, the unquenchable optimism of this couple) and a flask of whisky which he placed with exaggerated tenderness in among the nappies. He began to load the car in the driving rain.

It was at this point that the five-year-old, who had been absorbed in writing a story at the kitchen table, announced that she too had a sore throat. Sure enough, it proved to be as red and raw as the others', and her forehead was hot. This is undoubtedly the moment at which we should have aborted the mission, and I opened my mouth to say so. But just then I happened to glance at her essay. It began: 'We are goowing fro ar holl'days AND I think ti will BE fun.'

I melted. I reasoned that they might as well all be ill in a caravan as at home. I missed the moment. And frankly, anyone with that degree of sentimentality on top of the terminal impulsiveness which launched the adventure in the first place, deserved the kind of holiday we ended up with.

Anyway, I phoned the doctor for advice and he said the latest invalid could share the penicillin until we got back. He wished us, without a trace of irony, a happy holiday.

So we set off in the driving rain, with one child convalescent, one confirmed ill, one heading that way, one suspiciously sneezy baby and – let's count our blessings – the family asthmatic rather smugly oozing health. Three-quarters of the day was gone already and we had a three-hour drive ahead.

'So. Seven hours after we planned to leave and by jove, we've made it to Anniesland,' said my husband, sounding just a shade brittle, as we parked outside the chemist to collect the prescription. 'I know. How about when we get there we unpack, then I'll have a cup of tea and start packing again.'

We got there in the end, and I would love to be able to report that we actually had a wonderful time. But let's face it, despite an idyllic location only a few yards from the beach, a wonderfully dinky caravan and the warmest of welcomes, the holiday turned out much as anyone with an ounce of sense could have predicted.

The sun, which had been making a few feeble attempts to shine for us, flopped finally into the slate-grey sea that evening and was never seen again. The rain became so torrential that we were trapped for most of our one full day inside the caravan, tripping over wet anoraks, sprawling bodies and muddy shells.

The children coughed and bickered, the baby – stuffed with cold and wind – couldn't sleep, the sea worked itself up into a most uninviting lather and the Monopoly money fell off the table once too often.

Oh, and I crashed the car. In a bid to lull the baby to sleep, I embarked on an unnecessary trip along miles of twisty single-track road to the nearest shop, returning with a tin of Heinz Fisherman's Pie for Infants and without a significant section of the car's bonnet.

23

Next morning we took all the linen back off the beds, packed the bags, loaded the car and limped home.

One day we'll look back and laugh. But maybe not quite yet.

October, 1995

Pregnant Problems

My friend Ruth is pregnant again. Two or three months ago, as part of an ongoing campaign to ensure that in ten years or so I'm not the only menopausal mother at the primary school gates, I told her she ought to have another one. This, she now tells me, coincided nicely with a 'wee notion' she had of her own.

It is a notion to which the mothers of three or four children are, I find, surprisingly susceptible. Logic would suggest that the more ghastly each pregnancy becomes, the more unendurable the symptoms, the more decrepit your poor, child-abused body, the more, in short, you know what it's like, the less likely you would be to want to go through with it ever again. But logic has precious little to do with the child-bearing business.

One friend has had five children in under seven years and is already calculating where she'll put the sixth. Another one has six already and explains: 'Yes, I know every pregnancy's got worse, but you see, every baby's got better.'

This is a common theme among mothers-of-many. Somehow, amid the discomforts and fatigue and engulfing mayhem of an expanding family, we manage to enjoy each baby just a little bit more than the one before. I'm sure this is because, being basically sane and rational folk, we are convinced from, say, number two or three onwards that this is the absolute last. We love it with all the passion reserved for a joy we know to be fleeting. Who understands better than we how quickly this soft, complaisant butterball will become a snotty, whingeing toddler?

Instead of urging this one on, as we did the first, to ever higher feats of development, agonizing over how long he's taking to sit up or crawl or hold a spoon, we revel in what we fancy are the never-to-be-repeated pleasures of infancy. 'This is the last time a tiny downy head will coorie into my neck,' we sigh, as the milky-breathed bundle snuggles into that nook in the shoulder which is made for babies. 'Never again will I see that gummy grin,' we sob when the first tooth appears.

Then, of course, we have another one. I suppose it's all that savouring of unrepeatable pleasures that compels you to repeat them. And so the process continues, until you finally call a halt when the husband threatens divorce or you realize you'll be drawing child benefit at the same time as your old age pension.

I dare say every woman would stop at one child if it were not for the almost total amnesia that sets in after the pregnancy is over. I imagine the propagation of the species would have all but ceased in this generation if any woman actually remembered afterwards what it felt like to carry a child for nine months.

As my friend Ruth moaned down the phone the other day, 'I don't know why on earth I ever have these notions.' I distinctly remember her saying much the same thing three times before. I said it myself. Once you're pregnant, you can't for the life of you re-member why you wanted to be. I recall being rather shocked once when a friend who was expecting a baby at last after two miscar-riages said from the depths of her nausea that she wished she wasn't.

But if you've never been there, or you're one of those lucky women who 'bloom' all the way through, it's hard to appreciate how awful it can be. I'm still close enough to the last one to remember the never-ending nausea, the foot-dragging tiredness, the superhuman effort of will it took to go to work, drag a trolley round Tesco's, feed the children, wash the clothes, monitor the homework, read some interminable Noddy bedtime story, climb in and out of innumerable bunks for cuddles and smile brightly at the unexpected guest who's turned up for the night – when all you want is to be sick and go to sleep.

Then there are the multifarious discomforts so casually dismissed in the medical books as 'minor irritants'. Cramps. Spots. Wind. Hair as tough as a lavatory brush. Tights falling down. People complimenting you on your nice, round face. Stuffed-up nose. Urine sample leaking all over your handbag (this one not in the textbooks, but ought to be on the grounds of the extreme psychological stress when you pull out a soggy chequebook in the supermarket).

Aware that we're suffering like this for an ultimately joyful reason and that many women who would love to be pregnant can't, we try to rise above it. We don't complain – much. Barely able to stand up under the waves of twenty-four-hour nausea, we refrain from hitting the midwife when she says kindly, 'Have you tried a dry biscuit first thing in the morning?' We part with £25 for arcane homeopathic powders. We wear silly wrist bands with bumps that are supposed to make contact with pressure points and ease queasiness. They don't. We either eat nothing at all or, in my case, have to eat more or less constantly to stop being sick.

(Presenting a morning television news programme and haunted by the fear of throwing up on the breakfast tables of the nation, I used to smuggle handfuls of nuts into the studio, stuffing them into my mouth when the camera was elsewhere. 'Magnusson's on the peanuts again,' the whisper would zip round the newsroom. 'Must be expecting.')

Who in her right mind would go through it twice out of choice, never mind three, four, five, six times? But nature's little amnesia ploy is so sneaky that within a few months of the birth (the horrors of which are also struck so fast from the memory that we can be describing it as 'not a bad labour' five minutes after ten hours of hell) we are already starting to wonder what all the fuss was about. My husband has learned to back away fast when he hears me musing about what's a little sickness, after all.

Thank goodness I've remembered again.

November, 1995

Daggers Drawn

My daughter was singing as she polished the furniture. I hadn't asked her to polish the furniture. I never do. But where one brother is happiest with a computer, one with a football and one with a model car, her idea of bliss is a can of Spring Fresh and a duster. Where have I gone wrong?

While the boys have to be nagged, bribed or tricked into doing their infinitesimal share of the household chores, and can't be seen for dust when they think they're finished, she's up on a chair with the Fairy Liquid before you can say 'dishes', scrubbing at pans as if her life depended on it.

Being a bit of a tomboy myself and not too hot on the domestic skills, I used to argue till I was blue in the face that the differences between men and women were all about upbringing and expectations. Nobody could have approached motherhood with a grittier determination that all children would be treated the same, not channelled along some pre-ordained path. Boys would be offered soft toys to cuddle, girls would play with cars and trains. I would breed the New Men and female engineers of the future.

I dare say there are indeed small boys and girls who do such things, but not mine. The hubris awaiting me was a family in which every politically incorrect stereotype in the book is rife.

Ten years ago, as I gazed at my first-born in his cradle, I fantasized about the gentle soul he would be. No guns or nasty aggressive games for this little peachblossom. He would be taught to turn away wrath with a soft word. His toys would all come from the Early Learning Centre. He would grow up to be Secretary-General of the United Nations.

The fantasy sustained me until he was about two, when he proudly presented me with his first Duplo model – a rifle. Later on, at playgroup, he and his pals daily assassinated each other with the creative output from the Sticklebrick table. In the garden he and his brother began doing such heart-stopping things with sticks that in the end I went out and bought them a couple of plastic swords.

We went downhill fast. A decade and three more sons after those early dreams, we now house an arsenal of swords, rifles, water pistols, bow and arrows, hatchets, daggers and tanks that would be the envy of the British Army. Not so long ago, we were all nearly arrested when a most life-like revolver in our luggage caused a security scare at Heathrow Airport.

I have now resigned myself to the fact that little boys simply enjoy aggressive games and love weapons. It's in them from the start. Mind you, I'm quite prepared to admit that my boys may be worse than others. I imagine, for instance, that my third son is probably alone in feeling that the working day has not begun properly until he has brandished a chop-stick at his nursery teacher. Nor is my once-cherubic first-born perhaps typical in his enthusiastic membership of the Scottish Amateur Wrestling Association.

But I think, all the same, that it's just a matter of degree. Cuddly and affectionate and lovable as they are when you get them on their own, small boys en masse provide a sobering spectacle for optimists about the future of the world. One wonders less at how many wars there have been through history, than at how few.

And what of my daughter, the lone sandwiched sister? Has the overwhelming presence of boys, train sets, guns and footballs in her life produced a tomboy? Not a chance, any more than the accumulation of dolls and Little Ponies and Polly Pockets has had the slightest civilizing effect on her brothers. She never knows from one minute to the next whether her favourite doll will be found strung up by the neck from her bedroom door or kicked down the garden to score the winning goal for Aberdeen.

She can hold her own all right when push comes, as it frequently does in our house, to shove. She can punch with the best of them and used to have a dangerous line in teeth. But the idea of fighting for fun, for pleasure, would never occur to her.

She plays all the boys' games because she has to. You'll find her from time to time teetering round the house in plastic high heels, with a handbag (pink) in one hand and shotgun in the other, and she can manage a tolerable dribble down the left wing when they need someone to make up the numbers. But her heart is not really in it. She would much rather be drawing or writing or cutting out stars or polishing shells or – dear heavens – cleaning the bathroom, while waves of boys surge and roar around her.

I finally faced up to the fact that boys and girls are simply born different on the day, a few years ago, when I was hanging out the washing and gave her and the next brother up a couple of clothes-pegs to play with. He shot me with his. She cradled it in her arms and sang it a lullaby.

These days, while they all love our real baby equally and with a passion, she at five is the only one I can trust to look after him for more than two minutes. The seven-year-old does his best but is easily distracted, the eldest's idea of child-minding is to birl him around in his baby-walker so fast that his head nearly spins off, and the second-youngest thinks there's nothing like a few swift taps on the head to cheer a baby up. She alone has the patience to sit picking up discarded rattles and replacing them time and again.

So naturally she is the one I tend to ask for help with the baby. She is also, in the throes of her current love affair with the duster and the toilet cleaner, the one who helps most with the house-work, while the energy required to pin a son down for long enough just to pick a biscuit off the floor makes it so tempting not to bother.

But I won't give up. I'll continue to try and treat them equally and expect the same of them. And by the time they're all in their teens, I imagine they'll be equally impossible to get to do anything. But right now nature is wearing down the nurture. Equality is hard work.

November, 1995

Ox One, Donkey Nil

By the time you read this, I will doubtless know the worst. Either my four-year-old son will have held his crook meekly at his side as humble shepherds are supposed to. Or he will have poked it in Joseph's stomach and subverted the entire nursery school nativity by playing the shepherd as some demented Power Ranger in a dressing-gown.

I will either be dizzy with relief or burning with shame. Either way I will be wishing he could have been cast as something nice and innocuous like his little cousin in London, who came home from nursery the other day to announce that he would be starring as a mince pie. My sister is having nightmares about the costume, but at least she doesn't have to worry about what he'll do with his stick or how to stop him lobbing the glowing embers of the shepherds' campfire into the manger.

This is always an anxious time for parents. More fingernails are chewed over whether fidgety angels will keep their wings straight or pint-sized narrators will remember how to pronounce Caesar Augustus than over just about anything since their first day at school.

My first experience of this festive stress came when our eldest made his stage debut several years ago as an ox. Resplendent in brown tights, a furry waistcoat and an extremely life-like mask that his father had been up all night making, he took his place on a step behind the holy couple and would have contributed to a very pretty tableau if the donkey had not also decided to strike a pose on the same step. Ox and ass then began to fight.

You can always detect the offenders' parents in these circumstances. While shoulders heave and giggles erupt around them, they are the ones either gazing with mute appeal at the stage or looking round self-consciously with an apologetic 'these-things-will-happen' shake of the head. In my case, I was also — if truth be told — willing the ox to win. The donkey, whom anybody could see had started the whole thing, had a sharp elbow and my maternal hackles were rising.

Eventually the infant teacher stepped in and separated the combatants. Everyone later agreed that it had been one of the most entertaining nativities for years.

The following year the occasion would have passed without mishap if I had not had to bring a baby to the afternoon performance. When he began to wriggle on my knee, I thought I would just let him crawl around for a while at my feet while the action proceeded on stage. How was I to know that the three kings were due to pass by my chair on their stately way to Bethlehem? Balthazar and Melchior made a deft detour round the baby and continued with dignity intact, but their pal never saw what hit him. His feet went and his crown clattered to the floor. We left hurriedly.

The next year our second son clocked up a family first: a speaking role. 'There is no room at the inn,' he yelled — they had been told to speak up — and I nearly expired with pride. Just as you always know at a glance whose children are playing up, you can also spot the proud ones at a hundred yards. Their faces are suffused with the most perfect, blissful satisfaction. It's not smugness, nor merely relief. I reckon it's the purest and most innocent revelling in the achievement of another that adults are capable of. I still go all gooey with emotion when I remember my tiny innkeeper, all bright-eyed and eager, delivering his one pathetic line like Henry V rousing his men at Agincourt.

Partisanship is, of course, the order of the day. I love the way that whatever the shortcomings, perfectly obvious to every other

34

member of the audience, all parents are secretly convinced that their little petal is the prettiest angel, the best singer, the sweetest shepherd (aaargh, shepherds – mustn't think of shepherds), the most handsome soldier, the juiciest mince pie. I also love the way teachers who have done it dozens of times before throw themselves into it like Trevor Nunn producing the *Hamlet* of a lifetime. And especially I love the magic that somehow escapes from mumbled lines and murdered tunes and battered haloes to invite you, compel you, to share the wonder of it all.

Christmas without wonder has always seemed to me a pretty hollow affair. It's not that you necessarily need to have children around, but there's no doubt that when they are, it's easier to catch the infection and discover your own capacity to marvel.

There is nothing guaranteed a bigger laugh in our house than to look back at a video we once shot of our Christmas festivities: the lovingly prepared festive table reduced to debris within minutes, the feverish toddler whose wails drown out the carols, the big, black rings of exhaustion round my eyes, the eternal squabbling over new toys, the dishwasher overflowing.

But there's a point in the video where we always stop laughing. It's when we watch the faces of the children carrying their candles through to the Christmas Eve table, singing 'Away in a Manger', and exuding that wide-eyed wonder that is the best part of childhood and maybe, if we can retain it or rediscover it, the salvation of our adulthood. It is a frame of mind that enables us to marvel at the actual claim of Christmas which, unless the central tenet of Christianity is completely off the wall, is utterly mind-boggling.

Children's minds are easily boggled by Christmas. What's a brawling ox or a dropped crown when you can touch the stars? Or, come to that, what's a delinquent shepherd on his last warning?

I will worry no longer.

December, 1995

Festive Blues

And so, as the baby yells himself to sleep, the dishwasher hums, the washing machine clatters, the US Cavalry in the shape of my youngest sister drives off to the pictures with the four eldest to see *Babe – the Gallant Pig* (we got our pork dinner in first, in case they're all vegetarians when they return), my husband languishes with flu in the bedroom (having managed to down a suspiciously large quantity of pork and apple sauce between moans), I sink into a chair at last and try to compose an article.

No. Wait. The baby is not yelling himself to sleep. The baby is merely yelling. I go up and yank him out of his cot and plonk him in the middle of the menagerie in the living room, which consists of my other sister and her three children, who are currently arguing about whether to watch Wallace and Gromit for the fiftieth time or go out for a walk.

Ah, a family Christmas. Nothing to beat it. Nothing like a few little ones around the place to spice up the festive period. This may well be true, but eight little ones, including four under five and our manic six-month-old puppy, may have been just a mite ambitious – the triumph of hope over the dark forebodings which my sister and I tried to suppress as we planned the jolly Christmas we would all have together: my five and her three under one long-suffering roof.

I don't wish to complain; we had our jolly moments. I particularly cherish memories of the present-opening session, where the abnormally huge load around the Christmas tree this year turned out to be due to the children having gone into toy-recycling in a big way. My entrepreneurial second son had even had the novel idea of recycling other people's possessions.

When the moment came, they swooped upon the presents from their siblings, tore off the paper with glad cries and lifted out the contents with baffled indignation struggling not to get the better of the politeness that has been dinned into them as the correct posture when receiving a gift. 'But these are already *my* books,' squeaked my daughter, restraining herself rather heroically, I thought. She turned to her brother: 'I'm afraid I've read them.'

The most successful present was a battered plastic castle with moving figures which the eldest had bought for 20p in the school bring and buy sale the other week, along with – as usual – vaster quantities of other people's junk than we managed to palm off on to their schoolfriends. The castle was duly presented to his second youngest brother and provided hours of fun for all the family, while the expensive Big Big Loader which is Big Big Trouble to assemble lay discarded nearby.

My favourite present, next to the little silver ring which my second eldest had blown his savings on, was undoubtedly the one from the four-year-old. This was a large cardboard box containing a blunt pencil and one baked bean. 'He got it off the floor, Mum,' reported his sister accusingly.

I seem to be spending the entire holiday picking up chocolate penny containers, washing clothes, washing dishes, hoovering up crumbs from the Sonic biscuits which Santa Claus in his wisdom dispensed by the sackful and drying coats, gloves, boots and scarves on radiators. While this is not a million miles from the usual domestic scene, it feels worse because a) there are an extra five people to do it for and b) I can't get out of my head the idea that somewhere or other in all this there ought to be a chance to relax. You know, sit down, drink coffee, indulge in sisterly gossip. The one comfort is that my sister and I are in it together. We've both opted for lots of children in quick succession and we know the score.

Right now I can hear her asking her husband if he would mind removing her three-year-old from the fire, as he appears to be sitting in it. A crescendo of screams from my seven-month-old suggests she's now trying to get him into his outdoor clothes to take him for a walk. Yes, there she goes past the window, bumping the pram over the snow and offering a cheery 'I've escaped the madhouse' wave as she passes. The menagerie now appears to have moved into the kitchen, from where I can hear one of my nephews shouting, 'Poo, poo, poo,' and my brother-in-law urging another one to eat up his beans or there'll be no Singing Kettle tonight.

This, then, is the intellectual environment in which I grind my thoughts into article-writing gear. And I'll have to be quick. No editor's deadline is half as menacing as the minutes that tick away until the return of four children, high on the exploits of a pig called Babe. This is the first few minutes I've had to myself since Boxing Day, when I locked myself into the loo for half an hour with a new book and remembered the times pre-children when the Christmas holidays were about reading and eating and walking further than fifty metres and watching old films on the telly and getting up late and having baths and playing Scrabble round the kitchen table until all hours.

Now all we do until all hours is try wearily to get children to bed and then spend half the night attempting to keep them there. Log fires are not for curling up in front of with a book; they're for keeping children out of. Books are not for reading; they're for gazing hungrily at, stroking the cover, sniffing the pages, gulping down the blurb and placing tenderly on your bedside table beside all the others you long in vain to devour.

Even beds are not for sleeping in any longer. Last night the baby cried from ten in the evening until three in the morning. Every so often he would burp, perk up, look dozy and scream again when I laid him down. I sat with him in the dark, profoundly regretting the magnanimity with which I had sent my husband to a spare bed to get over his 'feeling a bit fluey' symptoms (a common ailment in menfolk; women call it a cold) and I wondered how many women there are in the world driven to real despair by interminably howling babies. At one point in the night I screamed with him. He was so astonished that he stopped crying immediately. Eventually we dropped off together and in what we laughingly call the morning, around 6 a.m., he woke up bright as a button and ready for breakfast.

This afternoon, surrounded by my sisterly support system and fast-recovering husband (now, there's a surprise), knowing that however bad things get in the house I can always go out to work every now and then to get a rest, it's easy enough to smile at the rigours of the night and gird my loins for the next one. But for mothers on their own, stuck in the house with no help and no escape, a crying baby or a perpetually whingeing toddler must be well-nigh intolerable.

'Have you tried dropping him from a great height?' enquired my sister, who also has an active night-life. Black humour usually has a basis in truth somewhere and I'll bet there are more parents who flirt with the idea of child-bashing in the long sleep-hungry reaches of the night than society would care to admit.

Crunch of wheels on gravel. Sound of child falling out of car. Wails. Ah, the *Babe* party has returned. Will I go and say hello or stay here until I'm discovered? No, too late. They're coming. They're here, bursting in to tell me the highlight of the film was the moment when some child in the front row let rip with the most enormous explosion of wind and the cinema erupted in giggles.

I think I'll give up.

January, 1996

40

PART TWO

Family Extensions

There are some people who have proved impossible to keep out of these chronicles. Chief among them is my mother. After all, anyone who cannot be let out of the country without half-drowning herself in a French toilet (see p. 174) has to expect some coverage from time to time.

But the fact is that no account of our family life could possibly proceed without her. Since we moved back to Scotland and more or less on to her doorstep, she has walked the baby and fed the children and never failed to materialize when needed. She's collected the gang from school, taught them those mysteries of long division that remain a mystery to their mother, and laboured once more over projects on Roman Britain or the Highland Clearances which she must have hoped would never darken her kitchen table again. She's sung them her songs, rocking them to sleep with old Scots lullabies soft in their ears, and told them her tales.

They've listened spell-bound to the story of her own grandmother's family being cleared off their croft on the Isle of Mull to make way for sheep, gaping at the terrible truths about the Clearances, aghast to hear how landowners realized that one of the simplest ways of forcing reluctant crofters off the land was to take their precious cow away, then thrilling to the tale of how her grandmother's family cow missed them so much that it swam across the Sound of Mull from the place which is still called Calve Island and found its way miraculously back to the croft.

She's regaled them, too, with the story of her birth. She was the twin no one guessed was there, so jaundiced and emaciated when she made her surprise debut that when her father handed the midwife the two guinea fee and asked with sinking heart what he owed for the extra birth, the midwife sniffed and said, 'Oh, I'll just take ten shillings for that one.'

Any time now I expect she'll be moving on to the stories I was weaned on – her exploits as a young journalist in Scotland in the nineteen forties and fifties, first on the famously couthy *Sunday Post* and its sister paper the *Glasgow Weekly News*, and then on the *Scottish Daily Express*. I can practically quote by heart the poems she was obliged to produce every week on a *Weekly News* column called 'This Cock-Eyed World', which purported to be a letter from a soldier called Private Archie to his sweetheart Gladys, who looked after a barrage balloon in the WRAF. I'm not entirely sure why this required to be rounded off with a limerick, but it did, and desperation produced such gems from my mother as this:

A fellow who lived out in Yoker,
Hit his wife as she slept with a poker.
When charged with assault,
He said, 'It's no' my fault,
I thought that wee bang would have woke her.'

To mark the end of the war with Japan, she felt obliged to compose something with an oriental flavour. Since she didn't know much about Japan except the nickname of the Emperor, she was reduced to these immortal lines:

Most illustrious gracious Mikado,
No wonder you lookee so sado.
For, wee son of heaven,
As sure as I'm livin',
Most certainly it you have hado.

44

What made it particularly tricky was that you had to have the punchline in the last line. One week, totally stumped, she sent her column off to the head office in Dundee on the wire. Back came, by return, 'Mamie Baird has not sent poem.' She wired back, explaining that she simply couldn't think of one. Across came another wire: 'Must have poem by five o'clock.' So she sent them this:

A poet, a wee friend of mine,
Can never think up the last line.
He gets the first four,
And cannae get more –
See what I mean?

Never one to waste good material, my mother has been quoting these verses in talks ever since. Once, when she was speaking to an old folks' club, one senior citizen laughed so much that he wet the floor. He died about two days later and she was told he died happy because he had never had such a laugh in his life. It must be the way she tells them.

Later, her *Express* days yielded a crop of royal-watching anecdotes. There was the time she got her glove stuck in the doorbell of the young Princess Elizabeth's honeymoon home on Deeside, causing the bell to blare incessantly until a posse of engineers was summoned to silence it. And then there was the day she drove through her home town of Rutherglen behind the Queen and Prince Philip when they were doing their royal tour of Scotland after the Coronation of 1953. Everyone she had ever known was out on the streets that day, and at the great climactic moment when the Queen stepped out of her car at the Town Hall, discreetly followed by the *Express* reporter in her Sunday hat and white gloves, a raucous voice from one of the tenement windows above pierced the awed hush: 'It is *so* Mamie Baird. And to think I used to wipe her nose on my peenie at the back door.'

That same summer she met my father, a young post-graduate student who was penning some modest lines about the Edinburgh

Festival for the *Express* to help his vacation solvency. Spotting him in the office with his blond hair and hirsute chin, she nudged a colleague and asked, 'Who's the character with the beard?' When told his name was Magnus Magnusson, she giggled and said, 'Come off it, nobody's got a name like that.' A few minutes later, when she left the office to go for lunch, he set off in hot pursuit, claiming later that he was just in time to see her disappearing round the corner, closely followed by her bottom.

This is where my father takes up the tale. He was captivated by her freshness, by her open, merry, gleeful way of looking at life. He liked her eyes, and the way her nose crinkled when she laughed. But he was falling in love at the same time with her craft. She was the muse, the goddess of journalism, and he had become a devotee of both. He decided to abandon the dissertation on Icelandic saga manuscripts and apply for a full-time job on the *Express*.

Their backgrounds were totally different. She was a working-class girl whose father had been a wood machinist and then a school janitor, a passionate socialist with a love of learning he had never had the chance to indulge; she lived in a council house, helping to keep her widowed mother. He was the privately educated scion of one of the most bourgeois families in Reykjavik, living now in a big house in Edinburgh, his father consul-general for Iceland, his mother a glamorous hostess who had attended a renowned finishing school in Denmark and would have had a fit if she had known that when he spent Hogmanay that year with his beloved's family, the beer they had bought for him specially (this being a household which religiously brought the New Year in with ginger wine) had to be consumed from a jam-jar.

My father's stories about past family exploits stand up pretty well beside my mother's. To start with, his grandfather's mother was allegedly ravished by the dashing Crown Prince of Italy on a naval visit to Iceland. (Come to think of it, this one wipes the floor with the homesick cow.) The conclusive proof of this intimate family connection with Italian royalty is apparently that the baby born some months later boasted a head of suspiciously dark hair and a

46

swarthy complexion, a quirk in the blond Scandinavian stock that has been resurfacing ever since. My unimpeachably proper grandmother rather enjoyed the racy legend behind her luxuriant dark-brown hair and blue eyes, and I only need to look at my own youngest son – another dark-haired, sapphire-eyed stunner among four blond siblings – to think, 'Aha. Crown Prince'.

Then there was Laxamýri, a heart-stoppingly beautiful estate in the north of Iceland, rich in sheep, eider ducks and salmon. It was a place of glorious and lucrative abundance, built up by the family at the end of the last century but, in a long-lamented disaster, gambled and frittered away in the next generation by a clutch of feckless brothers. Or so the story goes.

One of these brothers became the great Icelandic poet and playwright, Jóhann Sigurðsson, my father's great-uncle, an impossibly romantic, Byronic character who wrote a poem that my father loves to recite, dreamily savouring the words which to him seem to sum up the wasted promise of the House of Laxamýri: '*Einn sit ég yfir drykkju / Aftaninn vetrarlangan . . .*' It ends with lines about Death bearing in his mighty hand the unfathomable night skies, poured to the brim with darkness – which always make him go all broody and Nordic.

The sister of those Laxamýri brothers, Snjólaug, had earlier been cast off by her father for falling in love beneath her station. She rode away on her shaggy-maned Icelandic pony into the sunset, leaving Laxamýri for ever, with nothing to her name but the few gold coins which her mother secretly sent after her. She married her humble suitor, who eventually became the eminently respectable fire chief of Reykjavik. Their four daughters were the fêted belles of the city. One of them, Ingibjörg, was my grandmother.

She proceeded to fall for Sigursteinn Magnússon, my grandfather, who was the son of a man they called Magnús the Carter, a crofter whose main claim to fame was that he owned the first four-wheeled horse cart in the northern township of Akureyri. Sigursteinn's uncle, Jóhannes from Borg, was the strongest man in Iceland.

This is all rollicking saga stuff, and your eyes are popping by the time my father has finished describing how this great-uncle Jóhannes of his could carry a grown pony on his shoulders at the age of eleven, how he became the wrestling champion of Iceland, how he used to do exhibitions around the world with a troupe of young men bizarrely dressed as cowboys and Indians, and how he eventually managed to beat the great German wrestler Schumacher, or Beefenbacker, or possibly Hackenschmitt (my father is a bit vague on names) on the roof of New York's Madison Square Garden.

These Icelanders don't just tell the sagas. They live them. At Jóhannes's eightieth birthday party, he challenged my father to a wrestling match. My father was a stripling of twenty-five and rather full of himself as a judo enthusiast; Jóhannes had angina. When the young man hesitated, thinking that he'd probably kill the old boy, Jóhannes glowered at him, like a Viking of old, and demanded: 'Answer me yes or no. Are you afraid to wrestle with me?'

My father looked him in the eye and forced himself to answer 'Yes.' And Jóhannes gave him a strange look back. Was it disappointment at his cravenness, or relief at his diplomacy? Either way, there was a glint of unholy glee in the old man's eye, because Jóhannes from Borg, by hook or by crook, had won, as he always did.

I love these stories. I could listen to them all day, and frequently have. One of these days when the Nintendo is off for long enough, I'll pass them on to the next generation, who at the moment chant *'Takk fyrir matinn'* after every meal, call their grandfather 'Afi', celebrate Christmas the evening before their friends and retain bracing memories of a summer holiday traipsing across lava-fields, without having a very clear notion why.

I'll tell them about Sigursteinn and Ingibjörg getting married and having a son named Magnus after the Akureyri carter, whom they brought to Scotland at the age of eight months when Sigursteinn was appointed European manager of the Icelandic Co-operative Society. I'll tell how they set up home in a large house in

Edinburgh with a maid and a nanny, and how Ingibjörg was very beautiful and sweet-natured and made perfect pastry the way she had learned it in the Danish domestic school, but that she never quite mastered English. To her dying day she always said 'vee' rather than 'we', placed her fruit in crystal 'bowels' and inquired fondly after our school 'chumps'; she regularly baffled the butcher by asking for three 'libs' of sausages.

I may then mention that Magnus's parents doubtless thought at first that he could have done better for himself in the marriage stakes than the harum-scarum reporter from Rutherglen and were disappointed that his university romance with Princess Astrid of Norway hadn't got very far, but that Ingibjörg took Mamie instantly to her heart and overlooked the fact that her daughter-in-law couldn't have told a Danish pastry from a Swiss roll.

Which brings me back to my mother. While her husband began a swift ascent through the ranks of the *Express*, she left to go and have babies. He only married her for her job, she says. She never returned to work, although for a while she kept up a flow of free-lance articles about such matters as life with toddlers and the perils of carefully coating your daughter's first birthday cake with icing before baking it in the oven.

Her mission was to devote all her energies to motherhood in exactly the same way as she had thrown herself into twelve years of journalism. None of her daughters has followed such a clear-cut path, but as we frantically juggle the complex ingredients of life in the nineties, we can't deny that her way worked. Our childhood was presided over by a mother who had reached the top of her profession, beaten the men at their own game without even trying, and far from feeling trapped in some arid domestic cul-de-sac was plainly relishing the challenge of what to her was simply another and even more demanding career – motherhood.

She has embraced grandmotherhood with equal relish. On hearing that the birth of my first child was imminent, she arrived on the next plane from Glasgow and proceeded to breathe and pant her way through a vicarious labour on my living-room floor while I was getting on with the real thing in hospital. Between us we got the baby born at last, and when she arrived to inspect him, she looked as exhausted as I did.

Willing me successfully through labour was only the beginning of her ministrations. In the years to come there were babies to be burped and bathed and blethered to, miles of floor to be walked with the latest tightly swaddled bundle, endless renditions of *Dream Angus* and *Shoo Shuggy O'er the Glen* to be crooned.

When she went home after each birth, I became a telephone counselling junkie. Whatever the moan – a child who wouldn't sleep, or wouldn't eat, or who, in the memorable case of my first-born, insisted on conducting relations with his reception class teacher from under the desk – she could always rustle up some advice. Even if it only amounted to 'Hang on in there. Let the baby cry. This stage will pass,' it was all that a novice mother needed to hear. Thus emboldened I was able to hurl the Penelope Leach handbook, with its exhausting child-centred prescriptions, a very long way across the room.

These days her own house is once again throbbing with children. My youngest is at this moment stuffing himself with pasta at her kitchen table so that I can get on with writing this. Tomorrow my pregnant sister descends with her three for the weekend. Our youngest brother, who hasn't graduated to children yet, has left his cat there instead.

Not that my mother copes with it all on her own. Her twin sister, she of the two guinea birth, joined the household a long time ago to help look after us all and, to our great good fortune, stayed. We did rather well for mothers after that, having gained a second while continuing to enjoy the full attentions of the first. Anna still reigns supreme in the parental home, a popular supplier of Wee Willie Winkie sausages, chips and beans to all itinerant grandchilden. Of her many accomplishments, the ones currently in demand from the youngest visitors include shooting down passing aeroplanes with Rice Krispies and marching round the house with a diminutive baseball cap perched back to front on the top of her head barking, 'I'm Officer Kidlington. I think the fire's that way, Fireman Sam.'

The third member of this family rescue mission is my father, who welcomes all comers with open arms and then beats a hasty retreat to the study. He has not, to my certain knowledge, ever changed a nappy or found himself able to remain in the room while such an operation is in progress, but if the grandchildren want to know the difference between a hawk and a kestrel, or why Gunnlaugur the Viking would not limp while both his legs were the same length, then he's their man. He is the great-hearted, brooding strength at the core of the household.

So let no one say the extended family is dead. It may not be what it was in the days when grannies and aunts and uncles and hands-on neighbours lived up the same tenement close as you, or just around the corner, or down the next street. Today's grannies may be required to hop on an EasiJet shuttle rather than the number 39 bus. But the point is, it still happens. Families do still muck in to support one another. One generation is still doing its bit for the next.

And that generation still has stories to tell which offer a bit of perspective and romance to the next one. I mean, it's nice to know you're descended from the Crown Prince of Italy, the strongest man in Iceland, a family with extraordinarily clever cows and a ten-bob twin who broke the Queen's doorbell. It gives you a sense of identity.

Our Dairy Bread

Many years ago, before we had children of our own, we were invited to dinner with friends who gushed, 'Why not come a bit early and see the little ones in the bath?' Why not indeed? We made a mental note to be as late as we possibly could.

It was an early insight into a phenomenon with which we, from the other side of the fence, are now only too familiar, as are our child-free friends: the antics of other people's children are charming, amusing, clever and interesting in more or less exactly inverse proportion to how charming, amusing, clever or interesting their parents think they are.

Worst by a long way is parental pride in the offspring's musical accomplishments. Piano recitals of 'Für Elise' and, even more horrendous, the contents of *My First Violin Tunes* have been known to bring a wince of pain to the faces of even the most partisan grandparents.

But running a close second are undoubtedly the verbal felicities that drop from the mouths of other people's prodigiously talented babes. Who among us has not felt our eyes glazing and our attention wandering as infant witticisms are recounted in soppy detail by breathlessly admiring parents?

On the other hand, what parent among us has not regaled colleagues or friends with some immense profundity from our own infant's mouth – even in my case to the extent of boasting that the baby has managed 'ba-ba-ba, wa-wa-wa' three weeks earlier than the health visitor said he would – only to become uneasily conscious that the information is not making the mark you expected?

These nuggets also transfer notoriously badly to paper. Infant babble especially loses something in phonetic translation; in fact it loses just about everything that ever made it interesting. So I'll spare you any more of that. But I did think I might mention the huge pleasure to be had from listening to children exploring language. And since it's mainly my own I listen to, I warn you now to be prepared for glazed eyes. You can even turn the page right now and I'll never know.

If you're still with me, let me confide that one of the most memorable moments of our Christmas was when my daughter, who had been eating her tea in unusually thoughtful silence, piped up, 'Why is Susannah expensive?'

I panicked. Had the *Grange Hill* storyline become more than usually unsuitable?

'Well, we keep singing "Susannah is expensive", so I just wondered,' she added. Eventually we got the tune out of her and it turned out to be 'Hosanna in excelsis', a line I will never be able to sing again with quite the same solemnity.

She has also banished for ever the banality of the hymn 'While shepherds watched their flocks by night'. 'Why,' she asked earnestly one day, 'were the shepherds wild?'

The other day she announced, with the air of one who has made an important connection at last, 'Bread's good for you, isn't it? And so is milk. That's why we pray for our *dairy* bread.' The logic of this was so entrancing that I could hardly bear to put her right. When I do correct her six-year-old malapropisms, it is always with a pang of regret. A world peopled by expensive ladies and wild shepherds and bread from the dairy is so much more vivid than the prosaic alternative I have to offer instead.

These pictures are often so deeply embedded in a child's imagination that most of us can remember the words and phrases we got wrong long after the end of our own childhood. My mother has never forgotten the pleasure she used to derive from singing lustily about a teddy called Gladly, my cross-eyed bear. She invented a storyline for him, fantasized about his infirmity. 'Gladly my cross I'd bear' has never had quite the same power for her.

Someone else was telling me that every time she heard the word 'Henceforth' from the pulpit, she saw a flock of chickens marching across the farmyard.

It's no coincidence that so many of these are from our biblical heritage. The archaic sonorities of King James and the hymn-writers are probably the only language our children still encounter at the age of six that has not been levelled down to a patroniz-ing colloquialism; and doubtless even those will be gone soon, ground down in the relentless pursuit of relevance and instant comprehensibility.

Children revel in the richness of language they may not fully understand, English or Scots. They enjoy repeating the phrases, curling them round the tongue, making pictures in the imagina-tion. So what if their mind's eye sees hens sallying forth and squint-eyed bears? The meaning will come in time; the resonances will remain for ever. For what is a child profited if he shall gain the whole world of nineties-speak and lose his imagination?

Children are also rather good at reinvigorating our tiredest clichés. When my eldest was about three, I apologized for losing my temper. 'Oh,' he said, greatly interested. 'Where did you put it?' Around the same time, his father suggested he shake hands. Looking faintly puzzled, he obediently waggled his fingers in the air.

Three is a great time for language. At that age, they delight in experimenting with new concepts and feeling their way into metaphors to express ideas. My daughter came in from the garden once to tell me she was making a round square. 'A round square what?' I asked. 'A round square triangle, of course,' she replied pompously, as if explaining the obvious to a complete fool.

Sometimes they get it absolutely right and manage to express an insight of their own with complete felicity. At the same age, one of her brothers sat in the car one day listening to the weeping melodies of a violin concerto on the radio. 'The music's crying,' he told me pensively. 'Does it need to cuddle its mummy?'

Another time I switched from heavy rock to Radio Three, which was playing something by Mozart. 'Oh, it's lady music,' he exclaimed in delight. I began to think I had a budding Rachmaninov on my hands – something which, as his piano teacher will now attest, just shows how wrong you can be.

January, 1996

Run, Rabbit, Run

In the beginning was the rabbit. We called him Bunjy, for no better reason than that the rabbit down the road was called Bunjy and peer pressure starts early.

I had been waging a long anti-rabbit campaign, on the basis both of principle (I hate to see animals in cages) and weary prescience (no matter how fervent the promises to the contrary, I knew who would be responsible for excrement removal and there was quite enough of that in my life already).

What the children really wanted was a dog, but they accepted the argument that it would be unfair to get one until we lived on a quieter road. The rabbit-lobby grew apace, however, fed particularly by son number two, who was doing a pets project at school and complained vociferously – and, as I later discovered, quite mendaciously – that he was the only child who had nothing to show the class. He was not seduced by the offer of one of the great fat grey slugs who rampaged through our kitchen every night, nor of a rather sweet worm from the flower-bed.

It was only when he began to ask in all seriousness for a snake, a notion that his father didn't seem to find as ridiculous as I did, that my implacable opposition to rabbits began to weaken. Perhaps, I reasoned, we had a little Gerald Durrell in our midst and I was cramping his vocation.

So one Saturday we all trooped off to the garden centre and chose a tiny brown baby rabbit with whom even I fell instantly in love. We patched up all the holes in the garden fence so that he could run free and he was soon leading the life of Riley, hopping in and out of the kitchen, paying an occasional visit to his hutch for snacks, cropping what was left of our lawn when the footballers had done their worst and conducting what appeared to be a hugely satisfying homosexual relationship with the rabbit next door.

Our budding Gerald Durrell took him proudly to school in a box and never paid him the slightest attention again. But my cage-cleaning nightmares never materialized because Bunjy thoughtfully created a latrine at the back of the garden at the point where his fence met his lover's; he spent so much time there I nearly offered him the Sunday supplements. If ever a pet rabbit was in paradise, he was. Then we moved house.

At first it was fine. He missed his friend for a while, but was soon enjoying the run of the garden and the fields beyond, embarking on a hectic courtship of the local ladies and turning up at the back door from time to time for dinner.

Then, one summer's day, when he was pottering happily round his estate, munching a nasturtium or two, his nemesis arrived. A great black hulk bounded into view and tore across the garden towards him. Bunjy escaped by the merest whisker, and his life has never been the same since. Neither has ours.

His tormentor is our seven-month-old Gordon setter, accepted into the household to honour all the ancient promises of which we were clamorously reminded as soon as we moved house. Of course, we knew that dogs and rabbits are not Nature's most intimate buddies, but we thought we could get them to socialize if we started on the puppy early enough. We were wrong.

Every time the door opens she is out like a black bullet, hurtling round the garden in pursuit of her prey, yelping ecstatically as she catches the scent and streaking off in hot pursuit. Up ahead you can just spot a brown shape nipping under the fence and heading for the hills. The shaves are becoming closer and closer as the dog gets bigger, faster and stronger; she is even showing nascent signs of strategic thinking. For a while, like Tom and Jerry, the rabbit could adopt the simple expedient of popping behind a bush and watching smugly as the enemy tore past, slithering to a halt a hundred yards further on with a look of perplexed chagrin on her face. Now she's wise to that trick and halts in a flurry of legs at each possible hiding place en route. Bunjy now escapes by fluke alone.

A friend who is a leading light in Greenpeace came to stay recently and, during one memorable chase, shed about two pounds trying to head off the dog. He worried about the rabbit all weekend. The joiner nearly fell off his ladder with shock when the pair sped past him the other week; he later confided his opinion that that rabbit was not long for this world.

Something had to be done. Clearly we had a major territorial dispute on our hands between two free spirits with an equal right to be there. We tried controlled introductions again, but the rabbit nearly expired with fright. We made sure the dog's Pedigree Chum wasn't the sort with rabbit in it, in case she got a taste for it. We eventually decided that both of them would have to give up some of their cherished freedom.

Thus began a regime whereby Bunjy, to his disgust, was kept locked in his hutch while the dog was out. The dog was then locked in the house while the rabbit was allowed to hop around his little pen, which is surrounded by netting strong enough to keep him in but not the dog out. Then the rabbit would be put in the hutch again and the dog let out.

This regime quickly came to dominate our lives. The house would be rent with cries of, 'Who let the dog out? You can't do that – the rabbit's out!' – followed by the thunder of feet as the entire family poured into the garden and started chasing the wretched animals until we got at least one back inside. It was like something out of the Keystone Cops.

You'll have noticed the past tense. I think we were all secretly relieved when Bunjy burrowed under his netting two days ago and made a bold bid for freedom. He was never made for a hutch. Neither we nor the dog have been able to find him. I can only hope he's having a relaxing holiday a couple of fields away and has not met with a more lethal set of teeth than our daft hound's. The hound in question is now miserably bored.

Go well, Bunjy. We're rooting for you.

January, 1996

Menaced

Ah, there's nothing like the country life. Sun glinting on hill, burn gurgling, spring in the air. Just the sort of day to summon the dog, wrap up the baby, stride out with the pram and fill your lungs with great gulps of nice fresh radon.

Until we were bombarded recently with scary warnings about the possible dangers of living near pylons, I had barely noticed the things. If anything, I found them a rather comforting sign of civilization.

We might not run to sewers and gas pipelines, but some doughty predecessor of Scottish Power had made it up here once upon a time, up the road with potholes so deep you can paddle in them, over the burn and across the fields, to bring us light and microwaves and the *Nine o'Clock News*. If we thought of power lines at all, it was merely to regret the blot on the view from the bedroom window.

This was a common feeling. Fifteen years ago, when the newspaper I was with at the time sent me northwards to report on one of the last pockets of habitation in Scotland to be connected to the National Grid, I remember looking at those awesome giants striding across the Highland moors and trying to compose some clever first paragraph about the march of progress. It seemed like progress then. The inhabitants were rejoicing at being able to watch *Coronation Street*. Nobody was complaining that the lines ought to have gone underground. Nobody imagined they might be welcoming a deadly cancer-inducing gas into the back garden.

And maybe they were right not to imagine such a thing. Today's doom-mongers may have got it all wrong. The pylons may be as innocent as daisies. Nobody seems to know for sure, and it will doubtless be years before the research can prove it one way or another. But in the meantime yet another menace has clutched at our hearts, yet more angst to complicate the decisions we make for our children.

When our family lived on a road in England so busy at times that you were nearly asphyxiated by traffic fumes just going up to post a letter, I used to worry endlessly about the effect it was having on one son's asthma. I dreamed of transplanting him to open spaces and fresh air. We managed it at last, and now I wonder if I've bequeathed him leukaemia instead.

Food is another area fraught with unanswerable questions. When the salmonella-in-chicken scare was at its height a few years ago, I dutifully moved the family on to beef and pork. Now, in deference to mad cows, we're back on chicken and off beef, except – illogically – for trips to McDonald's which I haven't had the heart to ban, although I wish I could watch my children stuffing themselves with Quarterpounders with a fraction of John Gummer's complacency.

I thought we were safe with pork until a German research student told me a hair-raising story the other day about the antibiotics they feed to pigs. Nor have I been able to serve sausages with anything like equanimity since the time I made a television film about what goes into one.

Before I start getting sniffy letters from pig-breeders and beef-producers and electricity companies and anyone else who wishes to take issue with my gullibility, the point is that I'm not claiming to know one way or the other. Most parents don't. We're buffeted all the time by conflicting theories. From the moment our children are born we spend every waking moment trying to do our best for them, seizing on the latest available advice and following it to the letter because we would never forgive ourselves if we ignored it and they suffered. Then suddenly the goalposts are carted off down the field and we're suddenly on the wrong side.

Sometimes the consequences are tragic. I've just finished reading Anne Diamond's book about the cot-death of her son Sebastian, and found it almost unreadably harrowing in places. Like her, I and my friends all put our precious babies to sleep on their tummies, airily silencing our mothers' doubts by quoting the expert advice of the time. So invincible was this theory that I remember being quite shocked when my mother told me that we had all slept on our backs; I felt we must have had a narrow escape. Now we know different.

Poor Anne Diamond must live for the rest of her life with the agony of having followed the wrong theory. And who knows what else we mothers are doing now that will turn out to be quite wrong in a few years' time?

Nothing is straightforward any longer. When my first-born turned six months old, I fed him ordinary cows' milk. Now the orthodoxy says babies must be on breast or formula milk until they're at least a year old. So the current nine-month-old regularly yells the place down while I continue to boil kettles for his SMA, casting a longing look the while at the nice, easy bottles of milk waiting in the fridge. This morning I thought 'Sod this' (sorry – 8 a.m. is a stressful time in our house), and gave him the cows' milk; then spent the next hour feeling guilty.

Would my first-born be finding maths easier today if I had fed him different milk at six months? On the other hand, maybe someone will discover in a year or two that formula milk is lacking in some vital ingredient present in ordinary cows' milk. We hapless mothers wait wearily for the next tablet of stone to be handed down from on high.

Remember the summer of the apple-juice scare? Those of us who were delighted at finding a drink that offered lots of Vitamin C without turning their teeth black, and poured it down their throats at every opportunity, were suddenly informed that a particularly nasty chemical had rendered apples unsafe.

Remember the broccoli horror? That was the story about there being so many pesticides on vegetables that it would require, as I recall, ten full minutes of washing to make them fit for consumption. Vegetable preparation time in our house went up by about half an hour that day before laziness reasserted itself and I decided to let that one pass.

Then, just the other week, mothers who had been feeding their babies low-fat diets in a bid to set them up for what they kept being told was a healthy lifestyle were rapped over the knuckles by some expert or other who said what the infants really needed was plenty of chips. It's enough to make you weep.

Or laugh. If it weren't for the fact that it's usually the most grim and horrible diseases that we're threatened with, laughing the experts off would actually be the best policy. Certainly it's the only way in the end to preserve your sanity. But we care too much, we know too little, to laugh very loud or for very long. We can't forget that Anne Diamond's baby will never return, or that in some of Britain's pylon-shadowed places a lot of people have contracted cancer.

February, 1996

Supping with the Devil

I have a friend who has no television. Her three children are being brought up without it, and she has stuck to her guns over the years with a firmness of purpose that has induced in me both admiration, of the kind she inspired in my Pampers-thirled breast when she used to hang her towelling nappies out to dry, and a vague feeling of inadequacy.

All those times when I've hauled my hypnotized offspring away from Power Rangers and out to the sunshine, I've thought, 'We really must do it. We must get rid of this thing.' But of course, by the next weekend, the joy of not having our bed invaded at the crack of dawn while they hurtle down the stairs instead to immerse themselves in pap is simply too seductive.

I also lack the moral courage to remove the lifeline of the video recorder, which is the salvation of many a rainy day, a refuge for sick children and a handy device for keeping the wee ones occupied when the toys have palled and the siblings are still at school.

I'm not sure, mind you, that banning the telly has any great effect in the long run. My husband was denied one in his early years because his parents thought this newfangled contraption was vaguely sinful and might explode. So he spent his time lapping up *The Lone Ranger* at his pal Howard Thompson's house round the corner and dreaming up excuses to visit old Mrs Gent down the road, who was also bravely supping with the devil. He is still at his happiest channel-cruising late at night with the indiscriminate appetite of one who once starved.

The argument for banning it is that children who are not watching television are likely to be doing creative things like painting and pressing flowers, while those who *are* watching are likely to have their spoken English corrupted, their minds anaesthetized and their morals undermined.

While the latter may be true if they're allowed to do too much of it and at the wrong times, it has gradually dawned on me that most of the creative activity in this house is actually inspired by television. This, of course, is entirely a reflection on my utter hopelessness at the sort of crafts modern mothers are supposed to spend jolly afternoons encouraging their children in.

I can't make playdough, I haven't the patience to understand the instructions let alone make the wonderful objects in *A Hundred Things to Do on a Rainy Day*, I can't draw a horse, I can't bake ... in fact, I'm the sort of mother who, when it was my turn to help at playgroup, used to be relegated to putting the kettle on for the staff coffee-break.

My daughter, who at six has been a better artist than me for some years, was once so baffled at my unsuccessful attempt to draw an angel for her that she burst out: 'You can't draw much, can you? Just a Christmas tree, a heart and a house.' Desperately trying to think of something I *could* do, I ventured diffidently: 'I can write stories.' She pondered that one, and reflecting sadly on the previous Sunday's parable of the talents, commiserated gently: 'A Christmas tree, a heart, a house and writing – God didn't give you very much to be able to do, did He?'

So the only stimulus my children have had from me in the direction of crafts has been a sort of cheerful, 'Right, why don't you all do some painting?' Or, 'How about collecting some leaves and we'll, er, look at them and think of something to do with them.' Naturally they ignore me.

But come Monday afternoon, something wonderful happens. Suddenly the house is awash with paints and newspapers and Plasticine and Sellotape and scissors. Empty boxes are hunted down, felt-tip pens are retrieved from the back of drawers, a house-wide search is instigated for the glue. For hours, with a brief respite for tea and homework, peace reigns as they create things.

We owe it to a marvellous programme called *Art Attack*, which has encouraged them to paint more, draw more, design more and make more than I've managed in the last ten years. When visitors comment on the walls festooned with children's art-work, I say modestly, 'Oh, just some things they made at home.'

Other programmes, like *Alien Empire* about creepy-crawlies or some of the great television forays into bird and animal life, drive them either into the garden or into reference books to find out more. Shows like *How 2* have them discoursing learnedly about principles of physics that never once occurred to me in years of studying the subject at school.

And forget education for a minute. It's fun to share television as a family. It's good for me, who if left to my own devices would watch nothing more than the news and an occasional *Pride and Prejudice*, to have to thole *Gladiators* and Noel Edmonds now and then, for the cosiness of all snuggling up and enjoying something together.

Of course we could all snuggle up and tell stories, and sometimes we do. 'Right, let's have a story,' I announce brightly, and the youngest ones immediately start careering round the room, the eldest slopes off to the Sega and before long the entire audience has evaporated. Mr Blobby at least holds the disparate ages together for a while.

I still take my hat off to those who bring up children without television and applaud the time and effort it must cost them. But these days I reckon that as long as it remains servant and not master, it's not something to get hung up over.

Same goes for the Sega, the awful computer game system that I resisted for years until I gave in at last in the craven hope of winning a quiet Christmas. It needs to be controlled, or else they would be zapping each other every hour of the day; and the four-year-old has now been removed from its orbit after claiming he was seeing monsters in his dreams. But once the older ones have had their fix, they're quite happy to go and play chess or, would you believe it, Happy Families, the latest card craze.

It's all a far cry from the stories I was weaned on of my mother's childhood with no toys at all except maybe a rag doll at Christmas, a book for a Sunday School prize and a scrapbook containing her Aunt Betty's rather frightening feather collection. The games were all make-believe, and seemed to involve a lot of playing shops, with hams and sausages made from bits of clay, strawberries and lettuce from the weeds in the back green and money from bits of old crockery dug out of the ground.

There was, apparently, no such thing as boredom in those days, or so I was always informed as a child when I couldn't think of anything to do. Which may or may not be true, but it certainly seems to be the case that children of that generation managed to have a lot of fun with very few props. They also survived without mothers devoting hours to arts and crafts.

These days playing at shops means selling toys to each other for a tidy profit, and children do seem to have lost the capacity to play with nothing. But as long as there's still a place for Mr Pint the Milkman and Master Dough the Baker's Son, I reckon that television and computers can be justified in their place.

Yes, I've convinced myself. I will feel inadequate no longer.

March, 1996

Dunblane, 1996

I was going to write something in the usual vein this week, something light-hearted about children. But I find I can't bring myself to do it.

It's a harmless enough pastime normally, to chatter on blithely about the trials and tribulations of family life. But how little it all seems to matter today, when real tribulation is still so close to us, when nothing much matters except to treasure what we have and hold it tight.

I've found myself wondering what it must feel like in these days for other people who have lost children, but in less grotesquely horrifying circumstances than a gunman in a school. The death of any child, in any circumstances, is the most terrible of pains. It's the tearing out of a part of your very being. It's the shattering of your life. It's the agony that parents carry with them to their own grave.

Does it make it any easier, I wonder, to suffer your tragedy in private, maybe meriting a line in the local paper, maybe not even that? I think perhaps not. For all that the overwhelming interest of the world in Dunblane's nightmare brought with it an army of prying cameras and insensitive notebooks, at least it was an acknowledgement that the loss of those children mattered, that the world cared.

Everyone who loses a child feels that somehow the world should have stopped. The very cosmos itself should be shaken to its foundations. How can people possibly be rushing to work and arguing about trivialities and caring about anything at all except the only thing that matters, that your child is no longer on this earth? Why are the stars not crying? Why is there still a sun in the heavens?

In this last fortnight the world has come as close to stopping as it ever does. Nobody rushed about very much the day of the Dunblane massacre without feeling how hollow all our preoccupations were. And if there was no great cosmic convulsion, everybody who heard about it that day, from Iceland to Singapore, probably felt there should have been.

And last Sunday, at least part of the world did stop. For a whole minute we breathed together as one, we remembered, we felt.

I hope that perhaps in years to come, the parents of Dunblane will remember the great tidal wave of national grief that embraced their children as something right and fitting, not invasive; as something that validated their feelings and honoured their loved ones. They may find, too, that the very publicness of their tragedy will spare them some of the small hurts that those bereft in quieter circumstances often have to bear.

No one will ever forget they had that child or talk as if he or she never existed. No one at a loss for something to say will ever cross the road or avoid their eye. No one in Dunblane will ever need to be taught in the future that a sympathetic glance, a hug or the merest touch on the shoulder are worth all the words we can't think of to say.

I wonder if there are not parents all over the country who, even as they grieve for the children of Dunblane, are silently screaming to themselves, 'What about ours? What about ours?'

To be mown down by a car or claimed by disease lacks the apocalyptic horror of Dunblane's tragedy, just as the loss of one child will never attract the same headlines as sixteen, but the effect on a single family will be the same. And there will be no help with funeral expenses, no counsellors on hand, no civic services anticipating their every need. The only memorial will be a gravestone.

Perhaps what we have all experienced with the grieving people of Dunblane will help us to deal better with other people's grief in the future. It has torn us open, peeled off the reserve which has always been such a handy lid on our emotions, allowed us to cry in front of each other without embarrassment. It has forced us to imagine our way into other people's pain and not to shy away from it or hide from it.

This has happened, I suspect, partly because of the enormity of the thing and partly because the imagining in this case was for many of us only too easy. It could so easily have been another town, another school, another class, another sixteen children and their teacher. We could not help imagining.

Men in particular have been prised open by Dunblane's pain — especially, though by no means uniquely, men with children of their own. The first generation of fathers to have had real hands-on experience of children, from the labour room, through the nappy-changing, to the night-nursing and the dropping off at school in the mornings, have responded in exactly the same way as the mothers. They have held their own children very close, and wept.

I don't agree with Matthew Parris, who wrote in *The Times* the other day of his irritation at men who could not control their emotions speaking of the Dunblane massacre in Parliament. I like the man enormously, but he has no children and it showed. We are not, heaven knows, a remotely Latin race and tears when they come mean something. I'm glad our legislators can cry, and our policemen, and our journalists, and our ministers and doctors, and the legion of men unconnected with Dunblane who have not been too buttoned up to allow their voices to crack and their eyes to redden when they talk of that terrible day.

As a nation we have done a lot of self-discovery since 13 March. We have looked into the abyss of what we as human beings are capable of and been brought face to face with our responsibility for the society that produced a Thomas Hamilton. But we've also discovered that we can cry together without shame and comfort each other without embarrassment.

The test now is whether we can keep our imaginations open and our emotions vulnerable enough to embrace the many less public hurts and less dramatic sufferings in our midst.

March, 1996

Dreaming of Sleep

Forget young and old, man and woman, black and white. There is another classification in the world, rarely remarked upon but just as stark.

I refer, of course, to the division between those whose children sleep, or used to sleep, and those whose children don't, or didn't.

I know I've written about this sleep business before. It's a bit like being on a diet and thinking of food all the time. You become obsessed by what you can't have. And having been up with the baby last night approximately once an hour, and then up for good with him at 5 a.m., I'm finding it hard to think of anything else.

I know what you'll be saying, you members of the My-Children-Always-Slept brigade. You'll be saying: 'For goodness' sake, why doesn't she leave the wean to cry? You'd think after five children she'd know all it takes is a bit of discipline.'

But my comrades of the night will know differently. This fellowship of the bleary eye and the uncombed hair, whose every second sentence is a yawn and whose every waking thought is of sleep, will be with me. They know this is not an art to be learned or practised. Infants either do it or they don't.

Mine don't. I must be the only presenter in the history of breakfast television who does the job to get a night's sleep.

The one thing that keeps me going is the pleasure, the sheer perverse joy of hauling my eldest out of bed for school and remembering the years I spent wriggling away from his cot on my stomach, like a commando in the dead of night, in a bid to escape that beady, insomniac eye.

He was three before he slept through the night, by which time there was another wailing banshee on the scene. But at least he has taught me that somewhere in the distance there is hope. I dare say by the time the current baby is refusing to get out of his bed until midday, I'll look back and think I dreamed all this.

Dream? Oh, for the chance. Believe me, if there is a technique for getting your baby to go to sleep, stay asleep and wake up at a decent hour of the morning trilling, gurgling and playing quietly with his rattles, then I would have found it. I have read *How to Get Your Child to Sleep Through the Night* so often, I know chunks of it by heart.

I've stuck so religiously this time to the chapter about only ever offering your baby a sip of water if he wakes that he is now addicted to H_2O and gags if you offer him anything stronger.

I've left him to cry so long and so often – this, according to my book, is a last resort but never fails – that I live in fear of the older children getting hold of the Childline number. 'How can you be so cruel, Mum?' squeaks his sister, when I tell her to ignore the crying. 'But he *needs* you,' wails another, twisting the knife deeper into the already quivering maternal heart.

Anyway, as a long-term strategy it simply doesn't work. After a few nights of prolonged crying he does think twice about yelling every time he wakes, but this only lasts until the next cold, the next tooth, the next bout of wind (and I seem to have been blessed over the years with the windiest babies on God's earth), and then we're back where we started. Even Cruella de Vil here can't leave a child to sob his heart out when he's in pain or discomfort.

It is very hard for those whose children have slept effortlessly through the night since they were a few weeks old to understand all this. I used to go round such friends asking, 'But what did you do? How did you do it?' – always imagining there was some trick that had eluded me.

Usually the answer is that it just sort of happened. This is generally said with a degree of humility, because the parents of sleepers have learned that if you value friendships it's as well not to boast in front of the parents of the sleepless.

After all, when you're tripping over yourself with tiredness, it's difficult to feel quite as matey as you should towards the friend who tells you that her (or just as often, his) child goes to bed at six-thirty on the dot every evening and sleeps till eight the next morning. Dear goodness, some babies even have to be woken in the morning.

Those lucky souls who do not display the proper humility in dealing with their afflicted comrades had better beware. The next baby could be different. And don't the rest of us all secretly wish it will be.

Some parents and grandparents do claim to have hit upon The Answer, usually something subversive like a tot of brandy in the milk, which they propound with evangelical zeal. That one never struck me as a good long-term bet, but believe me, no medieval knight ever searched harder for the Holy Grail than I have. Or was more sadly deluded in the end.

More milk before bedtime. Less milk before bedtime. A dummy. No dummy. More covers. Fewer covers. In my room. In his room. In my bed. In his own bed. Answering his every call. Ignoring his every call. Going to him, but not lifting. Reassuring but not touching. Singing lullabies. Stroking forehead. Patting back. Hissing, 'Go to sleep, you little wretch.' Bursting into tears and phoning mother.

I've tried it all. And still he wakes, still he cries, and still, no matter how broken his night, there is that moment around 5 a.m. when it dawns on you, with a sinking conviction, that this is him up for the day. There's the evidence: two eyes gleaming in the darkness, two sturdy legs making short work of the bed-clothes, the warm aroma of soiled nappy, the general air of infant preparing for the day's business.

What makes it bearable is the thought that I am not alone. All over the country, all over the world (give or take a few time zones), there are parents stumbling out of bed with their eyes half shut and an armful of eager baby, waiting for the dawn.

We are in it together.

April, 1996

Road Rage

For once, the BBC weather forecaster got it right. Seconds after he had issued the audience of *Breakfast News* with dire warnings of snow and sleet all the way up the west of Britain that evening, I had a private word with him.

'Look, we're supposed to be driving from London to Glasgow tonight. Would you advise us not to?'

'Oh, I wouldn't worry,' breezed my colleague from the Met Office. 'I doubt if it'll be as bad as the forecast.'

'But you've just given the forecast,' I pointed out.

'Yes, but you know what the Met Office is like,' he said enigmatically, and rang off.

It was that batty assurance that gave us the courage to wave goodbye to incredulous southern friends at 8 p.m. that evening, as snow flurried around us and began to settle prettily on the roof-tops. Loaded up with five children, including a vomiting baby – no holiday of ours is complete without somebody being ill – we pointed the lights of the car into the dusty white distance and set off on what had to be the Journey to Hell.

It was not the weather alone that daunted us. It was the fearful combination of weather, car and children.

As anyone who has tried driving anywhere with more than one child will know, no torment that Hades has to offer can compete with being trapped in a car with squabbling siblings for a journey longer than about half a mile.

Sometimes I sit in genuine admiration of the sheer inventiveness that can produce an argument out of nothing. My best yet is the five-minute-long spat that developed from the four-year-old's monstrous allegation that his oldest brother was looking at him. ('I told him to stop and he's still doing it. Look round and you'll see, Mum. HE'S LOOKING AT ME.')

We had a titanic eruption not so long ago which started with one child clearing his throat at one side of the car, followed by an immediate claim from the other side that he was being spat at. There followed a succession of carefully aimed coughs from both sides and wails from the sister in the middle that she was being showered.

If one hums a tune, another will feel obliged to start on a different one, louder, or on the same one, manically. Believe me, you never want to hear 'All Things Bright and Beautiful' again after it's been murdered in three keys amid the howls of the original singer and overlaid with snatches of 'Molly Malone'.

There is no such concept as companionable silence. Vacuums have to be filled, immediately, with anything. Half a minute into the journey to school the other week, my daughter (six going on fourteen) turned broodingly to her brother, who for once was looking quietly out of the window, and offered this opening gambit: 'You're always accusing me of being in love with someone.'

'I'm not.'

'Yes, you are. You did it again this morning.'

'No, I didn't.'

'Yes, you did. Anyway, I know who you're in love with.'

'I'm not in love with anyone, and I hate girls.'

'Yes, you are, and the whole school knows who it is.'

'Mum, she's doing it again. She's always saying I'm in love with someone.' (Dramatic pause.) 'She's making my life a misery.'

'Mum, he's hit me.'

'She hit me first, Mum. She's doing it again.' Scuffle. Wail. 'Right, you're going to get it.'

'You're both going to get it,' I yell, flailing behind me with my left arm in a wild attempt to skelp some knees, which in these strict

78

seat-belt days is the only part of the anatomy you have any hope of reaching from the driving seat. Of course, the knees I actually reach turn out to belong to an innocent third party, who starts up a complaining litany of his own. 'What did I do, Mum? I was just sitting here . . .'

And on, and on, and on. It's really quite alarming when you think of our roads being populated by drivers operating daily under this degree of stress. There is no road rage quite so terrible as the fury of a mother who has had to listen to one ridiculous argument too many. Have the police, who crack down so swiftly on anyone spotted with a mobile phone clamped to his jaw, ever considered confiscating a much more potent hazard on the highway – a carful of children?

Goodness, even before you turn the key in the ignition your nerves are completely frazzled by the monumental arguments over where everyone is going to sit. I have a friend who has bought a Renault Espace purely so that her three sons can sit one behind the other in three rows, an arrangement which means they can't touch each other, and operates according to a strict rota.

We have too many for that. Even though I now allocate the front seat on a Monday-to-Friday one turn each basis, there is still endless room for debate among the rest over who gets a window, who has to climb over whom to get into the despised back row, whose elbows are too pointy, whose school-bag is getting trampled. Once the youngest starts expressing a preference, I'm out of here.

On our way down to London at the start of the Easter holidays, we had these bitter recriminations at every stop, plus the full repertoire of sibling argument over everything from who got the pillows to who was the biggest cheat at cards. The co-drivers arrived in such a state of nervous exhaustion that it took us days to recover.

That's why we decided to drive back at night, and why neither snow nor sleet nor rain nor wind nor the grave shakings of heads among friends who clearly thought we were off ours, could persuade us to wait till morning.

Well, let me tell you, it was all right. It was as good a seven-hour journey as you can have with a car-load of children who, as you're passing Oxford, want to know if it's time to look out for the 'Welcome to Scotland' signs.

We owed it to three things: the baby was not sick, most of the children slept for most of the way, and my friend the weather man proved to be absolutely right. We left the snow and sleet behind in the south and bowled up the M6 under a crystal sky.

Maybe next time he'll let the rest of the nation into the secret.

April, 1996

Music of Love

I have a friend who is a music teacher. She is as well-balanced a person as you could hope to meet. And frankly, I don't understand it.

Why is she not a gibbering wreck? Why does her eye not wink uncontrollably with nervous tics? Why are her teeth not ground down to stumps? And how can she and the rest of her saintly profession return so blithely day in, day out, to a job that drives me batty in less than five minutes, namely teaching music to children. Or in my case, supervising their practice, which often seems to come to the same thing.

The torture of hearing the same note played wrong, in the same tune, in the same bar, every single time – waiting for it, knowing it's coming, praying it won't, then *aaargh*, there it is – is so exquisite it's a wonder it never occurred to the Inquisition.

Then there's the great climactic release of tension when the right note suddenly, at long last, does come along. 'Yes, yes, yes!' I cry in ecstasy. 'Do that again. Please, please, do it again.' Anyone passing our living room must wonder what they're missing.

All they're missing is the sight of a small boy waiting patiently at the keyboard while his mother dances and whoops like Paul Gascoigne after a hat-trick. A single B flat played in the right place, just once, can do that to you.

But why does it not have that effect on music teachers? If I had to go through that process with umpteen pupils all day, I'd be wrung out like a dishcloth, an emotional ruin. But then possibly, just conceivably, I don't have the right personality for the job. To be able to do it at all, it seems to me, you either have to be tone-deaf (which is maybe not the best of qualifications), or you have to button in your emotions so securely that you must very quickly become one of the tight-faced prunes whose image we all associate with music-teaching.

Or else you have to be a very gifted teacher indeed. And the amazing thing – well, I'm amazed anyway – is that so many of them are.

Take my pal Diane. She says when she's teaching the piano she simply has to call on all her reserves of patience, which are considerably greater than mine, so as not to become like the tartar she remembers from her own childhood who used to rap her knuckles when she played a wrong note and nearly put her off music for life.

It's worth it, she says, for the thrill of watching the pride and the pleasure in the face of a child who has managed to play a tune or sing a song alone. She never tires of enjoying their enjoyment.

Like all the good teachers, she derives huge satisfaction from enabling children to discover music and, through it, gifts they didn't know they had. These days she's teaching three-year-olds how to listen to music, how to spot what the instruments are doing, how to interpret it. She has them doing aerobics to *Carmen*. She has them conducting. She teaches them, thank the Lord, about the importance of silence.

And while I don't know how many afternoons of 'We are splashing in the puddles, splash, splash, splash' I could stomach, she somehow finds the stamina to wallow in imaginary puddles and swish in imaginary leaves till the cows come home, and her irrepressible enthusiasm encourages in every one of these children a great sense of achievement.

Our own piano teacher is another paragon. She has transformed my sons from rebellious lumps under their last regime, whipped into lessons by a mother who's determined they'll be able to take over the playing of 'Auld Lang Syne' at Hogmanay parties when I'm in the zimmer, into moderately capable pupils who occasionally drop their guard and admit to enjoying it.

Once again, it is her enthusiasm that is so infectious. She manages to combine an iron discipline with a *joie de vivre* so invincible that I wish she could bottle me some for the next practice.

Her greatest joy is the choirs she trains at some of the least advantaged schools in Glasgow. She takes children who can barely afford a school tie to singing contests and wipes the floor with the posh competition.

'I show them they can do it,' she says. 'They can sing, they can make music, they can be as good as anyone, and better. They get a real kick out of it and so do I.'

It's sad that when councils and schools are strapped for cash, specialist music teachers seem to be the first to go. The importance of their work is always being undervalued. Like sport, music can be one of society's great levellers; but if it's downgraded in the schools, it will become more and more the preserve of the pushy parents of the middle classes, less and less an opportunity for kids from all backgrounds to shine.

Meanwhile, this pushy parent will push on, dragging her offspring from Sega machine to piano stool and sitting, stressed out by their side, while they falter through John Thompson's ruddy *Easiest Piano Course*.

I will remove the baby from the top keys, where he likes to experiment *allegro fortissimo*, I will suggest to the six-year-old that she practises her recorder in another room, I will suppress the dawning realization that the tea is burning in the oven, and I will guide my not-so-budding Paderewski through the delights of 'Little Bo-Peep'. (A while back, his elder brother refused to play this one until it was renamed. The title 'Little Bo-Peep' has been scored through and proudly replaced with one that he considered more appropriate to a chap of his macho standing: 'Menace at Midnight'.)

I will do this with patience, with cheerfulness and with the calm, even temper which my children so admire. Or maybe not. Maybe I'll leave all that to the music teacher.

May, 1996

Three Cheers for St Clare's

It's not often that I think about my university degree. They don't get you very far in journalism and they're not a great preparation for changing nappies either. But it did just cross my mind last night, as I sank into bed and opened my current reading material, *Claudine at St Clare's* by Enid Blyton, that greater things might have been expected of a first-class honours in English Literature.

In a teetering pile beside my bed are the books I really want to read: the ones I started so long ago I've forgotten the plot, the ones that require more intellectual effort than I can muster by the time I've booted the last child into bed, the Christmas hardbacks still untouched, the Penguin 60s I can never keep my hands off in the bookshops.

Robert Burns and R. L. Stevenson biographies, P. G. Wodehouse, the David Guterson whodunit, Finlay J. Macdonald's beautiful Hebridean memoirs which I've been trying to find the time to re-read for months, William Boyd, Herman Melville, Katherine Mansfield, Kipling, Montaigne – they're all there and more, gathering dust along with the 1944 edition of Mabel Liddiard's *The Mothercraft Manual* (translated into Siamese in 1933), which I bought in a jumble sale in case she had some tips on getting babies to sleep.

All these riches, and on what do I lavish those precious few minutes before sleep engulfs me? Enid Blyton.

Actually I found the experience hugely enjoyable. It must be nearly thirty years since I last picked up one of the boarding-school series, and I could see at once why girls of a certain age are so comprehensively hooked. It's wonderful stuff.

It bears absolutely no relation to the way anyone lives, even at boarding school, I would imagine, then or now. But the irritating people who knock Enid Blyton for not being 'relevant' entirely miss the point. We loved those books precisely because they were like another planet, with just enough similarities to our own to enable us to imagine ourselves into all the best roles. We could lose ourselves in the comforting world of St Clare's or Malory Towers as completely as in Tolkien's Shire or Lewis's Narnia.

By the second paragraph I was hooked all over again. 'Fourth form,' said Pat. 'Golly, we're getting on, aren't we Isabel!' I never knew anybody who said 'Golly' or 'I say' or who talked about 'the hols' or used 'shall' all the time instead of 'will'. But the vocabulary was part of the mystique; one golly and you were in.

How I loved the idea of packing up trunks for school, of playing lacrosse (I was never very sure what this was, but it sounded fun), of opening up tuck boxes and planning midnight feasts, of planting stink-bombs in the French class and organizing high jinks in the dorm. Thanks to Blyton I, who was so far from being a ringleader in terror that I once shed a tear for our mildly persecuted maths teacher on April Fool's Day, could reign supreme in my mind's eye as the Naughtiest Girl in the School; she had a good heart really, of course, so it was all right.

The characters bore no resemblance to anyone I ever knew either. I used to scan my classmates for anyone as spiteful, sneaky, mischievous or high-minded as the Blyton pupils, but they never were, which made the books all the more attractive. And of course it was so comfortably predictable. Mam'zelle was always afraid of catching a measle, Bobby was never short of a trick, Hilary could be relied on to do the decent thing, the bad eggs were reformed by the last page and everyone moved on happily to the next class. Bliss.

I read *Claudine* last night because I wanted to see if the school sagas would appeal to my daughter yet, who has just reached that lovely stage where she can handle a whole book and is ready to try anything. I may not get a chance to read books for my own pleasure these days, but it's almost as satisfying to see my children doing it.

Mind you, it has been alarming to discover over the years that while you can lead a child to a book, you cannot necessarily make him or her read. I always imagined that if you surrounded children with books from infancy, read to them, listened to them reading, shared your own love of the written word, they would naturally become voracious readers themselves.

As with most fond maternal hopes, this turns out to be piffle. One of my sons lies in bed amid shelves groaning with all the books I've been collecting in my addictive visits to bookshops since the day he was born. He ignores them all and sticks his nose in *Beano* annuals going back to 1973, alternating with *The Adventures of Tintin*.

He has abandoned more books after one chapter, or even one page, than I can count. Why? 'It was boring, Mum.' He has always found reading easy, but simply can't be bothered with fiction. He would rather read up on sailing boats in the encyclopaedia than *Swallows and Amazons*.

Have television and computer games hijacked his imagination? Would he have persisted longer with *The Lord of the Rings* if he hadn't seen the cartoon version, which made the book seem unbearably slow? Does he simply have the sort of brain that prefers fact to fiction? Or is he – perish the thought – just plain lazy?

I'm coming to the conclusion that children simply are as they are. You provide what props you can and then have to leave them to it. Another son took longer to master the technicalities of reading but has an entirely different attitude. 'When I'm reading a book I enjoy,' he told me last night, 'everything else becomes a blur and it's like I'm somewhere magic.' Perhaps my bulk-buy of Asda bargain classics will be fingered at last.

But for Malory Towers and St Clare's I'll have to wait for my daughter. This is girls' stuff and she can't be ready too soon for me. Right now she's into Roald Dahl, who is the one author to have appealed to every one of them so far. His mixture of humour, subversion and fantasy seduced even my *Beano* boy.

But soon, I trust, it'll be Daphne and Gwendolyn and Claudine and Carlotta and the bell ringing for tea and lights out in the dorm. Or at least it had better be. Surely she wouldn't deny her mother the pleasure of collecting them and sharing the fun all over again. Surely she couldn't do that to me.

Oh well, the Montaigne essays can wait a bit longer. Hang the degree. I'd better get on with St Clare's myself, just in case.

May, 1996

Operation Night Out

My husband and I went to a dinner party last weekend. This, we calculated, was the first time we had been out together since last September. In saying this, I hope I'm not mortally offending some dear friend who entertained us royally between these dates and whom we've forgotten all about. Still, as we pointed the car east and squabbled about the quickest way to Edinburgh, we could not remember having done this for a very long time.

Nor could we remember ever, in ten and a half years of parenthood, having the prospect of an empty house to return to, something we owed to the felicitous coincidence of two children being invited to stay over with school-friends, two going off with my sister, and my mother gamely volunteering to complete the set by taking the baby for the night. And if you say it fast enough, it doesn't even sound like much trouble. Whoosh – children disappear, parents go out to play.

In fact, I spent half the day organizing the thing like a military expedition: washing pyjamas and drying shoes, collecting medications (calamine lotion for chickenpox, drops for a gooey eye, cream for eczema, inhalers for asthma) and then trying to remember which child currently needed them, hunting stray slippers, removing rock-sized chunks of ossified Colgate from toothbrushes, lining up five pairs of pants, socks, T-shirt, trousers, sweatshirt, Wellingtons and anorak and trying to match them up with the right toothbrushes and slippers in the right polythene bag.

The disaster of the eldest son ending up on the other side of Glasgow with his sister's pink polka-dot pyjamas would be one of such epic proportions for both of them that I checked the bags about six times.

Then I went off to hunt the baby alarm, baby shampoo, nappies, cream, spare vests, dummy, bottle and all the other paraphernalia required for one diminutive person to move a distance of three miles along the road for one night.

I dropped them at their appointed destinations, came home and tidied the house, loaded the dishwasher, fed the dog, collapsed into a bath, looked at the time, realized we were expected fifty miles away in less than an hour's time, hauled myself out of the bath and reflected ruefully that this was precisely the reason we hadn't been out together since last September. The effort nearly finishes you before the evening has begun.

But this time it was worth it, because for once we didn't have to worry about keeping the babysitter up late or start counting how many hours of sleep we would or wouldn't get before morning, if we stayed on for another coffee. These are thoughts not best calculated to make you the life and soul of the party.

No, this time we were free to accept another mint and hang the consequences. Refill those glasses and let's live, we cried. Actually, we had another cup of coffee and continued our discussion about post-modernism.

Now I have to confess, if there's one thing that having babies does for you it's to kill any previous interest you may conceivably have had in post-modernism, pre-modernism, post-post-modernism or any other sort of modernism. It certainly seems to kill the brain cells needed to say anything intelligent about the subject. Indeed at some stages in the maternal cycle, you're lucky if you can even pronounce it.

I first became aware of this phenomenon a few weeks after the birth of the first baby, when I was still reeling from the cataclysmic upheaval to my cosy little *ménage à deux*. I was invited to join the BBC's table at a glittering current affairs awards dinner in London. Someone else had probably dropped out at the last minute, but I

90

wasn't proud. This was my chance to slip back into the world of power-talk and in-house gossip and witty repartee from which a twenty-four-hour diet of crying baby and yellow nappies tends to distance you.

Just how far it distances you I didn't realize until, in the midst of the flowing wine and earnest analysis of the *Nine o'Clock News*'s running order, I was called upon to speak. Just what did I think of so-and-so's exclusive on *Panorama* that had caused all the controversy? Ah. Well. You see ... not only had I missed the programme and never heard of the controversy, but I took a full minute to remember I was talking to the editor.

In the course of the evening it transpired that I had seen nothing worth watching, had no funny anecdotes worth recounting that didn't involve babies, and could not come up with a single opinion on anything that anyone was talking about. What's more – and this was a heady realization – I didn't care.

At one point I heard myself wittering on to the head of News and Current Affairs about twenty-seven-hour labours; I may even have dropped in the word 'forceps'. I had a sudden vision of that story about the woman who, after many years of child-rearing, hosts a big dinner party for her husband's boss. Her bid to impress is somewhat dented when she finds herself leaning over him as she chats and automatically cutting up his meat. This is my future, I thought.

And maybe I was right. Ten years later, as the conversation rippled around me again, this time full of 'isms' and artists with names that ended in 'ski', I found I simply could no longer be bothered with the intellectual games I used to think I could play with the best of them.

I'm not sure whether to be discomfited by this – there are shades here, if I'm not careful, of the ladies retiring with a pat on the head to discuss Willie's measles while the chaps get on with important ideas over port and cigars – or to believe that it is women's earthier grasp on reality and more acute sense of the ridiculous and the pretentious that make us care less about lots of things as we get older.

Anyway, without getting too pretentious about it, we had a

most pleasant evening. We returned home around 2 a.m. and I crept around the dark bedrooms, stroking empty pillows and wafting kisses in the moonlight. Post-modernism, schmodernism, I thought, looking at the creaseless duvets, listening to the silence, wishing they were here. This is what matters.

June, 1996

Intellectually Neutered

So, with one fell column, I've set back the cause of women in the workplace, projected all mothers as brainless nerds and even incurred the sneers of my fellow columnist J.P. Leach for implying that motherhood is 'blissfully sweet and intellectually neutering'.

Far be it from me to pursue unseemly inter-columnar wars, but a girl has her intellect to protect. Come off it, J.P. Unless you're suffering a spot of neutering in the upper echelons yourself (and maybe fatherhood does that to you, old son; don't let it worry you) how could you possibly come away from my domestic chronicles with the idea that life *chez nous* is blissfully sweet?

As for the neutering bit, well, it may be that I exaggerated the damage to the old brain cells. This is what people do when they're laughing at themselves. But since at least one correspondent seriously thought I was saying that having children 'renders women incapable of having opinions', I probably ought to explain myself. In fact, I do believe I feel an opinion coming on.

For a start, I don't believe for a single second that motherhood robs women of their ability to think, reason and hold opinions. As a matter of fact, I believe more or less exactly the opposite, and I'll come to that in a minute. But it is undoubtedly true that the business of looking after small children, twenty-four hours a day, is draining. It exhausts mind and body. Bliss? Get real, J.P. It's hard, hard work, and your mind is so numb sometimes you're hard pushed to remember your telephone number. You do daft things. You wonder if you've got the early symptoms of Alzheimer's.

I almost fell over a friend the other week who was kneeling on the pavement in front of her young son, giggling quietly to herself. The boy was looking faintly baffled. 'I just told him to wipe his nose with this, when what I meant was "Let me pull up your trousers,"' she said. 'My sanity's going.' I understood. Anyone who remembers what it's like with young children will understand.

I would also continue to defy anyone reeling from the fatigue and confusion of the early weeks of motherhood to sparkle at the dinner table. If by any chance you *have* managed this feat, do write in and tell the rest of us what you were on.

In acknowledging this and laughing at this, I am not undermining feminism, patronizing mothers or suggesting some terminal intellectual impairment. I'm simply describing the way it is for women trauchled by the early years of child-rearing. Nor am I even making a sexist point. Men who do the lion's share of child-rearing – or even, come to that, the merest mouse's share – also find it hard going. I dare say J.P. himself has been driven to distraction at the Leach tea table or found himself in less than his usual dazzling form after a night up with Junior.

But there's nothing like a good night's sleep in the short term or the maturing of the offspring in the longer term for rehabilitating your sanity, although I imagine the strain of wondering which brand of Ecstasy your teenager is being offered this weekend might still deflect your attention now and then from the giddier intellectual heights.

In the meantime, the adrenaline produced by the entirely different pressures of outside work can usually be relied on to restore the sharpness when you need it, whether you're controlling a classroom, manning a fraught checkout or chairing a board. Personally, I find that having to interview the Chancellor of the Exchequer about the finer points of the exchange rate mechanism before breakfast is as good a way as any of dredging the intellect double-quick out of the Weetabix.

But what I believe raising children does do is to undermine the intensity of your interest in, and your capacity for getting worked up about, all sorts of things that you may once have thought important. This is not a matter of the intellect; it is a matter of perception and perspective. You become less tolerant of cant and pretension, less impressed by intellectual posing, less keen to play power-games, less hypnotized by status, less 'driven' to achieve.

As a high-profile media friend of mine ruminated a few weeks ago: 'Do I really want my gravestone to say "She made some great TV packages about Bosnia"? Wouldn't I rather it said "She tried to be a great mother"?'

I've come across countless women who have gone back to work after their babies and looked with new eyes at the desperately earnest zeal of their colleagues in pursuing aims that just don't seem as important as they used to. Why should acknowledging this threaten women's position in the workplace? I would argue, on the contrary, that women who bring to that workplace the vast range of experience that having children involves, contribute a deepened understanding of life, a useful scepticism, a broader perspective. They usually have a better sense of humour, too.

Are such women 'intellectually neutered' because they can't for the life of them see the point in killing themselves to scramble up the corporate ladder; because the posturings of opinion-laden colleagues now make them smile; because clever-clever table-talk doesn't sound so smart to someone who's wrestling at home with a sick child or a dysfunctional adolescent; or because some 'intellectual' conversations teeter so ludicrously on the edge of pretension that the effort of getting involved in one is no longer worth it?

It's about shifting perspectives, that's all, and it's not exclusive to motherhood. It comes with maturity, with living a bit and struggling a bit, maybe suffering a bit. And it often leads to a reassessment of priorities too easily derided as sentiment.

When I came home late from that arty dinner party and looked round my children's empty bedrooms, I wasn't elevating some Waltonesque 'Goodnight, John-Boy' idyll over the world of ideas. I was actually imagining Jaymee Bowen's father, whose grief-haunted face had been in the news that day, standing in the room she'll never occupy again. I was thinking of the Dunblane parents who must still find it unbearable to look at those small untouched beds. And I thought of my own children and was grateful they were safe.

I was fumbling for the idea, familiar to anyone who has ever buried a loved one or held tight someone they thought they might lose, that what matters ultimately, when the talking is done, is each other.

June, 1996

Fishy Business

And so the fish season is upon us again – the season of galas, fairs, sideshows and diminutive golden trophies in polythene bags.

You see them everywhere you go on these obligatory Saturday afternoon treks round the latest local jamboree: the little bags of blameless goldfish dangling in the clutch of excited children, while appalled parents drag along behind, wondering distractedly where they'll put it, how much an aquarium costs and what the ruddy things eat, anyway.

I used to be adept at avoiding these snares, having been caught once and vowing never again. That fish expired after I dropped him and his bowl on the kitchen floor, and I have lived ever since under the baleful shadow of my children's suspicions that I deliberately lingered too long in picking it up. They might be right at that. If I've got to have fish in the kitchen, I'd rather they were on a plate.

Since then, there has been no one who could pick a more deft route than I through the local gala, avoiding any stall that looked from fifty yards as if it might be harbouring those swinging, glinting, tempting polythene bags.

But this summer my iron policing failed. The eldest wandered off on his own and returned with one of the dreaded bags. His siblings gave a whoop and raced away. By the time I got there, it was all over. Two more fish. A notice proclaimed cheerfully (have these people no mercy?) that goldfish would be available even if you didn't throw the hoops successfully. My daughter, who couldn't hit a target at two feet, was gazing ecstatically at her prize.

On the way home we bumped into a friend who offered us an old tank that had been languishing in the garage since his own children's goldfish days. I accepted with sinking heart. I could see it all again: a future of forgotten feeds and unchanged water, marauding dogs and murderous babies, all culminating – as sure as fish is fish – in ultimate tragedy and the pressure to buy another.

My husband, who enters much more graciously and enthusiastically into the spirit of these things, sprinted off to the garden centre and came back loaded with coloured stones, exotic foliage, a Pinocchio statue (a sort of piscatorial garden gnome) and every conceivable delicacy for the gourmet goldfish.

Then the arguments started. First it was names. You'd have thought with three fish we would have been all right, but we had reckoned without child number four, who returned from a visit to his grandma's to find three of his siblings in possession of a new pet. No, he didn't want one for himself; nothing as straightforward as that. He merely insisted that they all, to a man or woman, be named Tom Fish.

This is not a child to be deflected by considerations of mere convention or logic. He fought his corner with such tenacity that the others fell back and agreed to compromise. Thus were Flossie Tom Fish, Flipper Tom Fish and Chip Tom Fish formally welcomed into the household.

Then we had the arguments over feeding. In a reversal of normal practice that would have astonished the family dog and the lately departed rabbit, the competition that first week was over who had the superior right to scatter fish flakes into the tank rather than who had the best reasons for not doing it.

By the following Thursday morning the bickering had reached crisis point. The race for the fish flakes had brought two of them to the point of blows and I came racing down the stairs to threaten the direst sanctions if they didn't sort it out amicably.

I went back up to continue getting dressed, only to be interrupted again, one leg into my trousers, by more piercing screams from below. They had solved the dispute by handing the fish food to a neutral bystander, none other than four-year-old Mr Tom Fish himself, who had promptly emptied in several weeks' worth of the stuff at once.

I left them changing the water and stomped upstairs again. Two minutes later the house was rent once more by a succession of Oscar-winning howls and shrieks and the clatter of feet on the stairs. My daughter, who is well placed for a career on the stage at the best of times, staggered into the bedroom, sobbing hysterically.

'What is it now?' I thundered, stabbing myself in the eye with the mascara brush.

'My fish is dead,' she screamed, flinging herself on the bed in an attitude of hysterical abandon.

'Well, it serves you right,' I roared, rubbing viciously at a big black streak of mascara with my thumb and making it worse.

She'll remember it all her life, I bet you, the day her fish died; the first trauma in all her six years, and her cruel and heartless mother said it served her right. I don't suppose she'll remember the mitigating circumstances – severe provocation and a poked eye, m'lud – nor all the hugs and kisses afterwards, nor the way I overcame my feelings about fish to scoop it out with a tea-strainer and place it on a kitchen towel for her to indulge in one last, tender look.

But she may at least remember the funeral, a touching ceremony, although I say so myself, the gravitas of which was only slightly tempered by son number two rushing out to the garden just as I was asking God to bless this His little creature, and yelling at the top of his voice, 'Can anyone join the christening?'

We marked the grave with a piece of wood and a card bearing the inscription: 'Here lies FLOSSIE, beloved fish of A.L.S. Also known as Tom Fish', with the dates of purchase and demise, a pathetic five days apart.

She travelled to school in the front seat, so erect and noble in her grief that I half expected her to declaim at any moment that the odds was gone, and there was nothing left remarkable beneath the visiting moon.

She was diverted only by the thought that the teacher would undoubtedly want to hear all about it, as would the class, and by the time we arrived at the school gate, she had the story honed to a tee. She allowed herself to be led gently into school by one of her friends who, catching the spirit of the occasion immediately, placed one arm round her shoulder and took charge of her satchel. Girls are rather good at this sort of thing. Both were enjoying themselves hugely.

Later that day the bereaved one romped to victory in the school sports. Flipper expired the next afternoon and was flushed unceremoniously down the loo. Today only Chip Tom Fish remains, sole survivor of our day at the fair, basking in the shadow of his plastic Pinocchio and wondering, no doubt, why no one ever remembers to feed him.

July, 1996

Beyond the Pail

I have before me a blue bucket. There is nothing in the least distinguished about this larger-than-average plastic pail, except that it has now assumed a high-ranking place in the annals of our marriage, joining a boiled egg and a stubbed toe in our collection of long and ridiculous tiffs about nothing.

The question, as we stuffed the last child into a car already bursting with children and luggage, was whether this bucket should travel with us.

My argument, which was put – I felt – so lucidly, concisely and reasonably as to brook no logical opposition, was a threefold winner: there was self-evidently no room for it in the car; those children in the grip of a tummy bug could be sick into polythene bags if they had to; and (my *coup de grâce*) there would undoubtedly be another one waiting for us in our holiday villa.

Instead of falling back in admiration of such cool reasoning, my husband said rather snappily that he was the one who had packed the car, he had personally and with careful forethought made room for the blue bucket in front of the baby-seat, where it was providing a neat holder for the sandwiches, and (his *coup de grâce*) it was what the children were most comfortable being sick into.

I didn't think a bucket that two of them had been retching into all night was the best repository for the family picnic, and said so. Anyway, what was wrong with sick-bags? The poor mites didn't have enough left in their stomachs to fill a thimble, never mind a giant workman's pail. (The thing was getting bigger and bigger every time I looked at it.)

That, apparently, was not the point. The point, I was given to understand, was that I had no right to come wandering out to the car and take issue with his packing arrangements, which had taken him a long time and nearly cost him his head because the boot door is broken and keeps falling down, when I had already objected to the seating arrangements he had just, at heavy cost to his patience, negotiated with the children. He'd given in to me on that, but he was hanged if he was going to budge on that blue bucket.

Besides, he added somewhat lamely, you never knew when a bucket was going to come in handy.

The experience with the boiled egg early in our married life had taught me that this is not a man to be moved when an important principle is at stake. All I remember about that long and infinitely silly argument is that I was the one to give way in the end.

The point of the stubbed toe contretemps has also disappeared in the mists of time, but once again I must have come off worse because I do recall that same time later I was still sitting foolishly in the middle of a ploughed field waiting for him to come and look for me.

Flouncing out of houses with that very satisfying slam of the door is one of those little luxuries that you sacrifice with the advent of children, as is giving full and voluble vent to your feelings on the subject of blue buckets, at least when the said children are greedily drinking in every word. Still, I might just have got one withering retort in to clinch the argument if my mother, who was seeing us off, had not intervened at this point to say that she loved us both to bits but was glad she wasn't married to either of us.

My mother has a disconcerting habit of saying things to your face that should decently be whispered behind your back. This was so unanswerable that it shut us both up, and we drove off to the accompaniment of a tuneless chorus of 'We're all going on a summer holiday' from the back seat. The blue bucket came too. Naturally.

Our destination was Center Parcs in Sherwood Forest, where the bucket joined a shiny red plastic pail in the store cupboard of our rented villa and we joined the hordes of other holidaymakers pedalling their way self-consciously along the leafy lanes.

The absence of cars is a most beguiling feature of Center Parcs. There is nothing to beat the entirely unjustified sensation, as you whizz along with the wind in your hair, of being wildly healthy and sportif. Only our four-year-old, who had to be rescued from inside a bush at the bottom of his first hill and gently introduced to the concept of braking, was less than enamoured with the bicycle business. He soon settled for sharing the baby's trailer, a wonderful contraption like a bubble-car pulled by an adult cycle; the pair of them rode there all week like Chinese mandarins.

No break with a young family is ever going to be anything other than hard work. ('My Goad,' said a Glasgow women I met in the heavily populated laundrette, 'what a way to spend your holiday.') So I measure the success of these times by the quality of the moments – the half-hour here, ten minutes there – when you surprise yourself by actually feeling relaxed.

This time I look back dreamily on my Sunday morning cappuccino in the sunshine of the village square, reading the Sunday papers while the baby slept and the Westwood Welfare Black Diamonds Band in their smart black uniforms oompahed around me. I think of my seaweed spa bath; of cycling through the tangy pine woods one evening to the little cinema to eat popcorn in front of a silly film; and of standing one day in front of a lovely, quivering aspen tree long enough to understand why its leaves, mounted at an unusual angle on their stalks, flutter so nervously at the merest whisper of a breeze.

And I remember, as the unexpected talisman of our holiday, that blue bucket – never used, blocking the entrance to the store cupboard, where we kept falling over it, getting under everybody's feet on the way home, but already a legend in its time, to be dusted down with the memories in years to come.

'Remember the way we fought over that old bucket?' we'll say, perhaps, when we're old and grey and full of sleep. 'No idea why.'

July, 1996

A Spirit Crushed

Not many laughs this last fortnight. I went to a hospital near London to visit a close friend who had recently had a breast lump and her lymph glands removed. I found her curled like a foetus on her bed in one of those grim wards that seem positively designed to make you feel ill.

I was shocked by how utterly drained and beaten she looked. She had been home since the operation and had sounded quite perky on the phone. Yet after being in this hospital for only a couple of days, she looked finished.

Physically, it transpired, she was feeling not too bad; emotionally, she was wrecked. Two days before, still weak from the operation, she had been invited to turn up at 10 a.m. to learn the results of a scan. She waited all day. At 6 p.m. she was informed that she had cancer of the liver and four small brain tumours. She seemed to have no idea what the treatment would be, whether it was worth having, what her options were, where she would have it, what the effects might be. To just about all of the hundred and one questions I asked her, she said: 'I don't know.'

'Haven't you asked the doctor?' I kept saying. Oh, she had tried. But he was so dry, so distant, always in such a hurry. It wasn't that he was rude, exactly, just that he never looked her in the eye, never seemed to speak directly to her, just barked questions at the nurse over her head and grunted in reply.

'I kept trying to focus on the right question, but the next minute he was gone. In and out like a whirlwind. It happens every time I see him. I get so confused. He flusters me. Nothing comes out right. I think he's taken one look at that scan and consigned me to the scrap-heap. Three people have died in this ward since I got here. All I can think about is whether I'm going to wake up tomorrow.

'Am I going to wake up tomorrow, Sally? Will I be here in a few weeks' time? Can you look me in the eye and tell me that?'

I looked her in the eye and said, very slowly and wishing I knew more about the liver: 'I am absolutely certain that you're going to be here in a few weeks' time.'

She relaxed, even smiled a bit, and began to talk about other things. I sat there wrestling with my rage.

Who was this man who called himself a healer yet could so effortlessly turn an illness into a trauma and so casually crush a fragile spirit long before the body had done its worst? Do doctors like him have no imagination? Has familiarity with illness and fearfulness bred something worse than contempt? Has it atrophied their very humanity?

What had this man done? He'd done nothing. Precisely nothing. I honestly don't believe it would have ruined his schedule to treat her as an individual rather than the next in a line of diseased flesh, and encourage her to ask some of the questions he must have known were crowding into her mind. A couple of minutes spent looking directly at her, touching her hand maybe, goodness, even perching on the end of her bed, would have prompted her to burst out with the big question haunting her most: 'Will I die tomorrow?'

He could have made the elementary steps towards forming a relationship, so that she felt the person in authority over her, the person in whose hands she had been obliged to place her life, was someone she could trust. He probably feels he's done his job by diagnosing correctly and ordering the right treatment; the counsellors can do the rest. But he has left behind a shattered woman.

It infuriates me that it is always the weakest people, the least equipped to fight for themselves, who fare worst in hospitals. The articulate, the well-informed, the brass-necked, the ones with the money to go private or the backing of tenacious families can play the system. They ask questions, they complain, they shop around, they demand second opinions.

It is the quiet ones who suffer, easily intimidated by authority and paralysed by their own humiliation, confused by illness or age, too nervous to ask the things they have a right to know, often simply too fearful to formulate questions whose answers they dread.

These are the ones, like my friend with no one but a twenty-year-old daughter to support her, who find themselves at the mercy of grumpy doctors, the brusque, uncommunicative type, too busy to talk, too superior to explain, too dense to realize that bedside manners are the heart of healing, not an optional extra.

I know it must be hard for those harassed hospital doctors, who see dozens of ill people every day – none of them at their best, some of them querulous and slow to understand – to remember that each one is a human being with only one life that is infinitely precious to them and a spirit that can be bruised as easily as a butterfly by a steely reply or a curt brush-off. But if they can't remember it, they shouldn't be in the job.

Many, many of them do remember it. By the next day I had found another doctor, a respected cancer specialist in London, who was prepared to see my friend. Even down the phone he sounded so nice I nearly wept in relief.

He fitted her into an already busy clinic and assured her she wasn't going to die tomorrow. He answered all her questions and maintained, I suspect, a discreet silence about the ones she didn't ask. He reassured her that he had studied the proposed treatment and agreed with it.

As far as I can tell, he neither pretended everything was going to be OK, nor offered the sort of blunt prognosis she didn't want to hear, but she went away knowing that she hadn't been discarded on some scrap-heap of wasting flesh and that her life was valued.

This wasn't a private consultation or a less busy hospital. It was simply a kinder man, whose eminence, intellect and overloaded schedule have cost him neither his humanity nor his capacity to empathize with confused and frightened patients.

However much they try and teach bedside manners in the medical schools these days, I reckon it comes down to personality in the end. Unless we can somehow screen out the supercilious, the unimaginative and the cold-eyed before they hit the wards, the chance of being dealt with kindly when our lives are on the line will remain cruelly arbitrary.

The make-up lady at the BBC encapsulated the problem neatly when I asked her if she had had a nice weekend. 'No,' she replied. 'We had my nephew to stay. He's a medical student and he's so boring. Nothing to say, no interest in what anyone else is saying, no interest in anyone full-stop. God help his patients when that one qualifies.'

July, 1996

Postscript

My friend died a few days ago. She died in her own home, not many miles but a whole universe away from the hospital which forgot she was a human being. In the two weeks she was home, tended by a wonderfully attentive GP, a big, cuddly district nurse, a Macmillan nurse, a Marie Curie nurse, her own daughter and many friends, she was emotionally at ease and looked at times as near as you can get to happy when you know your life is ebbing fast.

When I saw her for the last time, supported by pillows in her living room, resplendent in a pink turban to cover her ravaged hair, I could hardly believe this was the woman I had visited that first time in the hospital. She looked terribly ill, that's true; but the twinkle was back in her eyes and she was laughing. She had lost the defeated look that had so appalled me before. The hospital was far behind her.

In today's post I found a letter from a doctor in Stirling who said she had been privileged to care for many terminal patients in the course of her work as a GP. 'Some time ago,' she wrote, 'while having a cup of tea with the family of a dying patient, his wife turned to me and said, "I suppose you get used to this, Doctor." The day I "get used" to human tragedy is the day I will hang up my stethoscope and go home.'

It was that kind of humanity that my friend found in her last days. It made the end of her life worth living and her death an easier thing for the rest of us to endure.

August, 1996

Humble Fish Pie

Time to eat humble pie again. I seem to spend half my life doing it. Never can a foot have been put down so emphatically and raised so ignominiously, quite so often, as mine.

Take this business of the fish, for instance. You may recall that despite my best endeavours and darkest forebodings, we took delivery of three ailing goldfish from the local fête at the beginning of the summer holidays. We had become, perforce, a fish-owning family. But I made my position clear. We are not entering a phase of eternal fish-replacement, I warned sternly that evening. Fish are trouble. When these things die, bless their little orange fins, that's it. No more fish. Understand?

Yes, yes, yes. They all understood. Only too well, as it happens. They understood that it would take merely two deaths, a few days of pointed comments about how sad and lonely the third one looked all alone in the tank, a deluge of offers to replace them with their own pocket money and several foot-dragging excursions past the pet shop, for their mother's iron determination to falter fatally.

Actually the killer blow to the resilience of their mother's will proved – and not for the first time – to be their father's will. He has this off to a fine art. I mean, who regularly frustrates my anti-Frosties campaigns by returning from the supermarket laden with not only Frosties, but Coco-Pops, Sugar Puffs, Honeynut Loops and any other cereal you care to think of that's positively bowing under the weight of its sugar?

Whose voice can be heard among the clamour of protests when I announce it's bedtime, suggesting with lethal reasonableness, 'Oh, why not let them stay up a bit longer . . . just this once?'

Who has subverted my excellent ploy of getting them to practise their times tables on the way to school, by introducing instead a points system based on how many animals they can spot out of the car window? The same cows, sheep, starlings and the odd pheasant are faithfully totted up every day. 'And what happens when you get all the points?' I asked the first time I was informed that tables were out and Dad's new scheme was in operation. 'Oh, then we're allowed a new aquarium,' I was told. This was the first I'd heard of a new aquarium.

When they look back on their childhood, they'll doubtless remember this harridan of a Frosties-denying mother, who nagged them about tables and kept telling them to hang up their coats and take off their shoes and eat brown bread; while beside her, basking in sunlit memories of sugar and ice-cream and late nights and fun, fun, fun will be their saintly father, the man who jollied along those dreary school runs with promises of aquariums and who trounced their carping piscophobic mother with the immortal words, 'But why shouldn't they have a few more fish . . . just this once?'

It would be nice to think I gave in gracefully. In fact, they all merely waited until I was away one afternoon and made a beeline for the pet shop. When I returned, the original fête survivor by the name of Chip had been joined by Snowball, Flounder and a mean-looking grey fish which our second youngest, the family eccentric, had named Mother Pot.

Since then, Snowball and Flounder have shuffled off this mortal coil and been replaced by another three whose names were never, I think, finally decided. There are also two algae-eating 'cleaner fish' called Dustpan and Brush, who lurk around sucking green slime off the sides of the tank.

Then only last weekend we emerged from the Viking Festival at Largs with yet another one. I suppose I should be grateful it wasn't a shark. Anyway, this makes, by my calculations, nine more fish since the day I put my foot down. Where will it end? The tank is being scanned hourly at the moment for signs of eggs. We are all supremely ignorant about the mating habits of goldfish, but there is a general feeling that there must be enough sexual chemistry in that tank by now for something to have happened.

Did I say tank, singular? Can I really have forgotten the house-wide raiding of piggy banks, money tins, ancient wallets and kitchen drawers that suddenly swung into action last week when Father announced that the requisite animal-spotting points had been achieved (aided at the end by the sighting of a hundred red cars on the way back from Largs – a big cheat, if you ask me)?

Off they all went to the pet shop and returned with a monster of an aquarium, now positioned beside the old one, which they can't bear to throw out and which will doubtless require several more fish to fill. Give us a few more weeks and we'll be able to open to the public as Scotland's latest Underwater Adventure.

But where the humble pie really comes in is that over the weeks, for all my grumbles, I too have been reluctantly beguiled. We all sit watching, entranced, while Mother Pot bullies her way round the tank (she's been expelled twice and is under suspicion in connection with one or two unexplained deaths), Dustpan and Brush hoover up the algae, and the ravishingly ugly black one flaps around the greenery like an imp in paradise.

The fish tank is still the first place the children rush to when they come down in the mornings. One son likes to draw up a chair and eat his toast in front of it, glued to the box. The baby's second word, after 'more' and before 'woof', was – wouldn't you believe? – 'ish'. As the family never tires of pointing out, these new members are a great asset. So why did you object in the first place, Mum?

It's hard to explain that, as with the pleas to have friends to stay every night, a snake for a pet, midnight frog-hunting expeditions and membership of every club they come across from karate to synchronized swimming, you say no to preserve your sanity. You have an exhausted vision of yourself eternally changing fish-water or stuck permanently behind a steering wheel or never being able to get to bed when you want to, and so you put your foot down and prepare for combat. But some battles are just born to be lost.

So I say 'No', then I say 'No' again, then I say 'Maybe', then I say 'We'll see', then – heaven help me – I say 'OK, just this once'. Then, of course, we all have wonderful fun doing whatever I said they couldn't. Pass the pie.

September, 1996

114

Songs of the Isles

In an undistinguished church hall deep in the heart of Bishopbriggs Martha Campbell was explaining that the roly-poly thing she was making with the playdough was an 'isbean'. I gather it was what we usually refer to in these parts as a sausage. 'By the way, what's the word for "playdough"?' she called over to Ruby Polock, who laughed and said they didn't have it on Barra when she was young.

It's weird to walk in on a children's playgroup in an urban street in central Scotland and find yourself transported to the middle of Uist or Harris – except that on Harris maybe the three-year-olds are more likely to be singing about Jamie's Boat and reading *Where is Spot?* than Bata Shemuis and *Caite bheil Spot?*

I had been invited along by a friend who has a child there. She is one of those folk who are rather sneeringly referred to these days as 'nouveaux Gaels', a Lowland Scot who has chosen to send her children to a playgroup and then to a school, also a smidgen south of the Gaeltacht, in which the medium of instruction is Gaelic. At first, mind you, she simply wanted the free transport to a school outside her catchment area; now she's a full-blooded believer and learning it at night-school herself.

The Auchinairn playgroup was a revelation: all those mites of three or four who had said goodbye to their mums in best Bishopbriggs English a few minutes before were now counting jelly babies in the tongue of the isles, singing about ducks going 'cuag, cuag, cuag' and chanting 'crogall mor, mor, mor' to the picture of a big crocodile on the wall.

Martha Campbell, a retired teacher from Kilsyth, finds helping at the playgroup a great way to practise the Gaelic she learned at night-school; she natters away to the children with an occasional glance at her vocabularly list and a wry aside to me to the effect that the trouble with Gaelic is that half the letters you don't pronounce and the words are a mile long.

The playgroup, like others in the central belt, was started by Gaelic-speaking parents who wanted to reinforce the language they were trying to pass on at home. It was the success of these playgroups that led to the establishment of Gaelic-speaking units in a handful of primary schools.

These in turn are proving such an educational triumph that more and more non-Gaelic parents are sending their children for total immersion in a strange tongue when they start primary school. If you think your four-year-old petal has plenty to cope with getting to grips with pencils and books and gym shoes, imagine having to do it without a word of English.

Amazingly, as I discovered at the Gaelic unit in Meadowburn Primary, also in Bishopbriggs, they cope just as effortlessly as at the playgroup. For the first two years of primary school they learn everything in the medium of Gaelic, studying the Oxford Reading Tree books with titles like *Kipper's Balloon* pasted over and replaced by *Calum agus am balun*, and Heinemann maths books with all the English bits similarly pasted over by volunteer parents. It must take for ever.

The infant teacher, Donalda McComb, blethers to her charges in Gaelic and before long they are blethering back. 'It's very satisfying when they come in August knowing nothing whatsoever of Gaelic,' she says, 'and by summertime they are away and becoming fluent. They adapt incredibly quickly.' I listened as she asked a couple of Primary 2 boys, who were making free with their elbows, what they were up to. The child's lengthy excuse in Gaelic contained several references to the English word 'punch'. In telling them both to behave, Mrs McComb slipped in the Gaelic word for 'punch'. 'That's how they learn,' she said.

Meadowburn opened the unit with government money in 1988 and now has fifty-nine children, and three teachers from South Uist. After two years of total immersion in Gaelic, the children progress to English studies, which I'm told they pick up fast because they already possess all the tools. They continue to be taught their history and geography and science and all the rest of it in Gaelic. By Primary 7 they are working at the same levels as the mainstream P7 class, but with one huge advantage: they are bilingual. They've also been given access to a whole culture, they've learned the poetry, the lore, the songs of Gaeldom, they've acted in Gaelic drama festivals, they've won medals at Mods.

It's mind-blowing to see how easily these children adopt a new language, switching to English in the playground and back to Gaelic at the classroom door with such effortless ease that it makes me want to scream at our scandalous waste of those years when children's minds absorb languages like blotting paper and the schools could be teaching them French, German, any of the tongues we struggle, too late, to interest them in when they're almost teenagers.

Not only are we passing up the chance to teach languages effectively, but we're missing the intellectual stimulus that bilingualism can provide. Immerse young children in a second language and all their language skills, indeed their very capacity to learn, seem to be expanded and strengthened. That, at least, is the prima facie evidence from the Gaelic units.

It's a pity there are not enough Gaelic-speaking teachers around for more of these units to be created. Already there are fears that if too many of the new education authorities try to start their own, the existing units will be diluted and the system start to collapse. That's sad, because these Lowland pockets of Gaelic learning can provide an invaluable education in a beautiful tongue and an ancient culture that has shaped much of our children's homeland; their minds are being opened to different words, different syntax, different expressions, all the different verbal music of another language; and they are gaining language-learning tools that will last them for life.

And let's not be too sniffy about the 'nouveaux Gaels' and their hunger for a language that belongs to other parts of our nation. Central Scotland's well-funded Gaelic units may be peripheral – laughably peripheral, some would say – to the survival of the language among Gaels in real Gaelic-speaking communities, but it's a language that still strums in the blood of the many Scots whose families left the crofts for the big cities generations ago; it's a culture we are all the richer for cherishing.

As I listened to some of the Meadowburn children singing the Gaelic songs they had learned for a recent Glasgow Mod, I thought of my great-grandmother sent away from Mull on the boat to Glasgow, to find work as a young chambermaid because her family was being forced off the land. As an old lady she used to sit in her kitchen in Rutherglen, weeping, as she sang the haunting melodies of the isles to her grandchildren.

I'm glad they're teaching them about that heritage in East Dunbartonshire.

September, 1996

118

Work Cure

If there's one emotion to rival a mother's passionate desire to be with her children all the time, it's a mother's passionate desire not to be with her children all the time.

It's this impossible equation that leads to such a state of terminal tension in the maternal breast. It's why we dream for months about a weekend away and then rush back after one night.

It's why we're daft enough to let our first evening out in months be spoiled by the memory of a tyrannical embrace at the front door and the preposterous question: 'Why are you *always* going out?'

It's why we slip happily away from domestic muddle and perpetual demands to do a day of what we laughingly call work, and then spend it wondering if the baby has found any more of the dog's worm pills on the carpet.

This is not the same thing as guilt, although heaven knows we're made to feel guilty about it often enough. It's more a sort of chronic ambivalence, which the dictionary defines as the co-existence in one person of opposite feelings towards the same situation – a complicated emotion which afflicts most of the mothers I know and not too many of the fathers.

When I begin to feel my sanity tottering, particularly on those days when the cupboard is empty, the baby is teething, the washing machine has broken and they can't mend it till Thursday, madam, the plasterers have barricaded the staircase, the dog has gone AWOL, the five-year-old asks me for the ninth time how to spell 'pongy poo' on the computer and the school phones to say one of the others has been sick . . . on days such as these I look forward to my fortnightly television stint in London.

I think of how I'll read the newspapers at my desk instead of in the bath or on the loo. I dream — since I'm on the subject — of going to the loo alone. I think of how I'll referee arguments about the state of the nation instead of whose turn it is to get the free gift in the cereal box. I think of wearing clothes that are not smeared with custard creams, snot or toothpaste. I think of washing my hair and having time to dry it, instead of dashing out in the morning looking like a demented lavatory brush.

Then, of course, the day arrives and I go and do all that. And yes, it's a most enjoyable relief. But can I wait to get back? Can I stop thinking about them all in the morning, wondering if their father has remembered to point them in the general direction of toothbrushes and clean clothes, if he's thought about the lunch money, the recorder, the wrestling kit, the football gear, the swimming trunks, the fireman's costume that one of them needs for a play, the letter explaining why another of them was off yesterday, the playtime snacks, the homework books, the thousand and one things that make getting out of our house in the mornings such a tranquil experience?

And I wonder whether they are all well. Was that cough starting to develop into something nasty? Would their father recognize the symptoms of meningitis? What if something happened and I wasn't there? Shouldn't I be there?

Not so long ago I swapped a shift and came haring home because the baby had a cold. His father who, as he pointed out rather tetchily, was coping perfectly well, was baffled at my sudden arrival at the front door like Florence Nightingale on speed, gasping, 'Where is he? Where is he?'

The child in question was sitting at the table plastering his face with a chocolate biscuit. He gave me a beatific smile and got on with it.

I tried to explain why I had needed so badly to see for myself that the baby was all right, to check it wasn't incipient pneumonia

('Don't be ridiculous'), even just to be able to wipe his nose for myself. But even the best of fathers can never quite see the point. They may miss their children when they're away from home, but unless there's a very good reason, it seems never to occur to them to worry.

Mothers don't need a good reason. Reason doesn't come into this. I would never step out of the door in the first place if I didn't believe the children would be happy and cared for in my absence. And they are. Life is a ball. Coco-Pop and Sugar Puff consumption in the household goes up several-fold. The baby overdoses on ice-cream.

It may not be great for their teeth, but I'm sure these short bouts under a paternal regime have been good for them. It's also been good for him (although I'm not sure he's entirely convinced), and it's good for me to have the chance to renew frayed stocks of patience. So why do I come rushing home at the first infant sniffle?

No answers on a postcard, please, because this balancing of home and away, reason and emotion, children and self, is too complicated to be glib about. We all do it differently, according to need or inclination. We frequently alter the balance as circumstances change. But what we all seem to have in common, home or away, is to wonder constantly if we've got it right. Biologically programmed to cherish our children, but no longer intellectually programmed to a lifetime of domesticity, no choice is easy any longer.

It doesn't help when women who have made different choices, or perhaps never had the luxury of choosing at all, sneer at the way others organize their lives. No tongues are more scathing than those of women criticizing the way others have chosen to tackle motherhood.

Parenthood is such a scary occupation: there are so many, many ways of getting it wrong. But there can be quite a few ways of getting it right, too.

I'll never forget visiting my sister a few months ago. She has three children under five and at that time could usually be found around teatime slumped at a table, whey-faced with tiredness, trying to keep her temper as she rammed food down her whinge-ing brood.

This teatime, though, she was bright-eyed and oozing patience as she coaxed the eldest to try one more mouthful, blithely ignored the toddler's whining and made aeroplane noises for the baby's every mouthful. Ma Larkin herself could not have presided more cheerfully over the teatime bedlam.

'How come the perfect mother bit?' I asked suspiciously.

'I went back to work today,' she cooed.

October, 1996

122

Au Pair Bonanza

We're infested. We're over-run. Everywhere you look in this house are au pairs, of all shapes and sizes, eating, talking, crowding out the kitchen, using up the hot water, phoning their families in far-flung lands, hogging the best seat in front of the fire and laughing too loudly at not-very-funny jokes on the television.

In the last fortnight we've had our last au pair from Holland plus wordless boyfriend, the last-but-two (another Dutch nymphette) plus travelling companion, a stray Icelander who was ejected from her last job and needed a roof while she looks for another, and our current saintly and long-suffering Icelandic au pair, who has given her bed to the homeless compatriot and – ten days later – is beginning to regret her hospitality.

We plan to apply soon for accreditation as Britain's first Refuge for Indigent and Travelling Au Pairs.

'At least,' my mother remarked, 'with all those strapping young people around, you'll have plenty of help in the house.' I rather hoped so, too, until the irritating truth began to dawn that a former au pair on a visit is highly conscious of her new status. She is a guest. She is no longer paid to scrape bits of tomato sauce-covered fish fingers into the bin and scrub congealed baked beans off the pan. Ergo, it will not occur to her to lift a finger. This is an interesting form of social hyper-correction, since any normal guest in a busy household would be leaping up to snatch the plates from the frazzled hostess and insist on doing their bit. I would find this phenomenon fascinating if I didn't want so badly to rub the fish fingers in their faces.

The homeless one has not been much help, either. She is, she tells us, feeling very depressed, and spends most of the day waiting palely by the phone for the agency to ring and drooping theatrically over the kitchen table. She eats pretty heartily, though.

We don't. Yesterday evening the children ate, the depressed Icelander ate, the dog ate, the guests ate, the current au pair got a little, and not surprisingly the chicken expired as we were serving. 'Don't worry,' said my husband politely, 'we'll get something later.' Worry? Not a chance. 'Poor things,' said last-au-pair-but-two, 'you'll have to eat bread.'

Since bread was exactly what we would be eating, the house having been comprehensively cleared of anything else, we didn't find that as funny as our guest did. She roared with laughter as she poured the last of the gravy over the last of the roast potatoes.

We had forgotten how disconcerting the Dutch sense of humour can be. They say things that we would find wildly impolite and not remotely funny, and then – depending on personality – either laugh uproariously or wait deadpan for you to acknowledge their wit. Although I love them dearly, it can be wearisome.

When they're not even trying to be funny, it's worse. I remember once driving a new arrival from the airport to our English home. Bowling along the motorway, I prattled on about local points of interest. She looked around with keen attention and remarked pleasantly, 'This is indeed a dreary place.' Even allowing for the aesthetic limitations of the M4, this is a bit of a conversation-stopper.

But, as I say, we're extremely fond of our au pair girls, past and present. You need plentiful supplies of resilience and good humour to survive for longer than a couple of days in this chaos of children, visitors and animals, and they've all had plenty of that, although we once had a blonde bombshell from Norway who used to complain about us in the pub to her local au pair circle. She longed for two children and an orderly lifestyle, and had clearly picked the wrong family.

124

I like to think we offer a useful training in Why You Shouldn't Settle Down Too Early. Girls come to us bubbling merrily about wanting to get married soon and have four children. They love the little angels, you see, and can't wait to spend their days doing fun, creative things with them. The awful reality of smelly nappies and bickering teatimes and endless washing is usually a dreadful shock, but they have all with varying degrees of enthusiasm risen to the occasion for the allotted few months. They leave with their career application forms firmly tucked under their arms – and it's rarely anything to do with children.

It also gives us a little dry-run on what our life may well be like in a few years' time, with boyfriends and telephones and deep hormonal glooms. One girl was simply incapable of getting through the day without at least three calls to her best friend – one to compare notes on the night before, one because she had nothing better to do, and the third to discuss clothes for the evening to come.

Fortunately the best friend only lived a couple of miles away, and the phone bill was nothing to the shock we got at the end of the first quarter after the blonde bombshell came to stay. Calls to the boyfriend in Norway amounted to some £200. Floods of tears, terribly sorry, she didn't realize it was so expensive, her father would send a cheque. It all ended amicably, but we were heartily relieved when she took up with a bloke living in the same town as us and was able to conduct the next sizzling romance on local rates.

To tell the truth, I take my hat off to these girls, one and all. They come to a strange country, with a language they are not always secure in, to a new family with all sorts of expectations that they do their best to fulfil. We have been fortunate in the ones who have come to share our bedlam. They've helped me to juggle increasing numbers of children and a career, to sit right now in a quiet study writing an article, for instance, in the knowledge that the baby will not have dismantled the video recorder while I'm out of the room and his siblings will not have punched the living daylights out of each other. That's worth a lot and I'm very grateful.

It's good that they come back, great that they still think of us as 'home'. Maybe it's even a compliment that the visiting ones would no more think of popping their sheets in the washing machine before they leave than they would in their own homes.

As I write, the second wave is preparing to depart, amid tears and promises to keep in touch. Soon we will be guestless, except for the drooping Icelander in front of whom I am even now plucking up the courage to place a bottle of window-cleaner and a cloth.

'Goodbye, goodbye,' I hear myself shouting. 'Come again soon.'

October, 1996

126

Hallowe'en

Time was when Hallowe'en was the merest hiccup along life's journey. After tea on 31 October my mother would produce a couple of towels and a sheet or two, we'd trail next door and say 'Whoo, whoo', offer a spirited rendition of 'I Belong tae Glasgow', collect a couple of apples and go home.

It has been a dreadful shock to discover that in the intervening thirty years or so, Hallowe'en has become a major production, a highlight of the social calendar, a source of parental stress, infant trauma and juvenile competitiveness, a time for parties, discos and relentless activity.

Last year, still basking in my ignorance, I sent my lot to the school Hallowe'en party in white sheets and tenpenny masks. They came home quivering with humiliation. 'It was so *embarrassing*, Mum,' the eldest muttered accusingly. 'Everyone else was in really cool costumes and I just had a sheet. When somebody asked who was behind the mask, I had to give another name.' It transpired that he had operated under the alias of the boy he liked least in the class for the entire afternoon.

This year, I was informed, things had to be different. Proper costumes would be required. Advance planning was the order of the day. With a week to go, the oldest ones set to work with a will, ransacking drawers, enlisting their father (whom they've long recognized as the only parent with an ounce of artistic flair) into making exotic masks, cutting holes in my best tights and disembowelling blameless pumpkins which, by the time Hallowe'en actually arrived, were in a state of miserably advanced putrefaction.

Then everyone forgot all about it again. All the different bits of costume were littered around the house and lost, the dog ate a skeleton glove or two and the turnip head also breathed its malodorous last. Whereupon come Wednesday night, just as I was swinging out of the house to see a press preview of *Long Day's Journey into Night* at the Citizens' for a radio programme I was doing the next evening, someone piped up, 'Remember we've to take our costumes to school tomorrow.'

I grabbed a bit of paper and scribbled a tender greeting to my husband, who was due to relieve the babysitter an hour or so later: 'Four Hallowe'en costumes required first thing tomorrow. Please prepare.'

Well, you have to hand it to him. This is a man who can rise to the occasion. I returned from three hours of angst and hysteria at the Citizens' to find the children miraculously in bed, the kitchen table laid out with four piles of ghoulish-looking vestments, and an extremely smug-looking husband asking if I'd had a nice evening. He pointed to a two-foot high witch's hat made from black paper and staples, brandished a broom scrupulously assembled from an old pole and a bunch of dead bracken, patted a couple of East Dunbartonshire bin bags cut into capes, and invited me to try on the plastic kitchen gloves emblazoned with painted skeleton bones.

Weak with admiration, I picked up the witch's hat. 'I thought he wanted to be a ghost,' I murmured. The smug smile got smugger. 'Changed his mind when he saw his sister's costume. No problem. All in an evening's work.'

And so off they trooped the next afternoon to the party. The school had thrown itself into the thing with some abandon: vampires, ghouls and bizarre cross-dressers – and that was just the teachers – rubbed shoulders with robots, pirates, skeletons, every species of Superhero and the occasional Little Bo-Peep. Our capricious witch took one look and announced he had never wanted to be a witch; he wanted to be Batman, and he wanted a sword. It was quietly pointed out to him that he could exterminate just as effectively with his wand, and that did the trick. He got started straight away.

As soon as they returned home, the eldest tore off the skeleton's costume and metamorphosed into a cool dude preparing to return to school for the Hallowe'en disco. My first-born. My baby. Ten years ago his bedroom was rich with the aroma of used Pampers; on Thursday evening it was ponging like a brothel with the heady scent of Lynx Deodorant Spray for Men. He had bought it himself. I nearly cried.

Then I sallied out to discuss arty things on Radio Three, leaving their father to explain to the other four – two witches, a second skeleton and the baby starring as himself – that he simply couldn't face traipsing up and down the village with a mushy pumpkin and a bunch of children who would go shy on him at the first door and leave him saying pathetically 'Trick or treat?' himself, like I had to do last year. He had a much better idea for a Hallowe'en treat, he told them.

Thus it transpired that as I was conducting an earnest discussion in Studio 4, Broadcasting House, about the writer Robert Bly's newly published diatribe against parents who damage their children's brains with 'the thalidomide of the nineties' (television), my own were happily comatose in front of two rented videos.

Anyway, it looks as if we've made it through the witching season this time round, and now there's only a daughter to be dressed up as a firework for her class assembly, a ton of wood to collect, a guy to stuff and a few cows to frighten with rockets before we're racing on to Christmas, three birthdays and then the school pantomime. But there's one thing that might ease the burden in the future. I thought I might start up a Parents for Old White Sheets campaign in time for next Hallowe'en. There's safety in numbers, folks.

November, 1996

Celebrity

I have been asked to donate a sock to a celebrity sock auction. That's right. A sock. I'm not sure whether to be wildly flattered or to succumb to the grave suspicion that someone is pulling, as it were, my foot.

Anyway, having looked into my sock drawer and hastily shut it again, I don't think pride would permit me to offer any of the sagging, off-black cotton numbers with the expiring elastic and the lived-in look that have served me so well for the last few years.

There's always the winter range in saffrons, scarlets and lime-and-crimson stripes that I've been hoarding since my mother went through a sock phase at Christmas a while back. But I was keeping these for the day that one of the offspring has to play Malvolio or maybe a neck-to-toe Joseph in some particularly vivid school production. And since they are as yet untouched by human foot (sorry, Mum), they might be deemed to lack the personal touch, although, frankly, I'm not sure how personal we're supposed to get here. Are we talking clean socks, for instance?

Then I thought it might be a novel twist if I offered the entire household collection of separated and divorced socks, whose partners have walked out in the sad and mysterious way that they do, stealthily, when your back is turned, never to appear again. They could auction the lot by the sackful, but I'm not sure it's quite what the organizers had in mind.

What did they have in mind, I wonder? With the greatest

respect to the good folk who came up with this wheeze, the whole thing is ridiculous. But it's only a degree or two more ridiculous than the normal run of celebrity auctions, celebrity toy exhibitions (you don't believe it? I have a letter on my desk inviting me to contribute something to a 'Toys of the Famous' exhibition in Essex), celebrity recipe books, celebrity joke books, celebrity art displays, celebrity poetry collections and a host of other reputedly stalwart fund-raisers.

What is this animal, the celebrity? And why is it that even in the land where everyone kent your faither and a man's a man for a' that, the beast is apparently valued so highly? You would think that after sixty years of television, the thing might be losing its mystique. You might imagine that when nearly everyone knows someone who has clapped to order in a studio audience, or been solicited by a roving microphone in the High Street, or phoned in an opinion to GMTV, or at the very least supplemented the chorus in *Songs of Praise*, we would all be more blasé about the professional players who strut their stuff on the television stage.

Yet if anything the cult of the celebrity is growing. No charity race, ball, fête or sale of work, no event of any kind that craves a bit of publicity, feels secure without a name for the poster or a 'face' on the podium. Is it really true that we're less likely to put our hands in our wallets for a cause that hasn't received the stamp of approval from some character who happens to read the news for a living, or attend an event that hasn't commandeered the support of a soap star or two, or vote for a political party that doesn't parade the allegiance of half a dozen actors and a footballer?

Even as I write it, I have a dull feeling that this may in fact be horribly true. Or at least the organizers of these things think it's true, which is almost as bad.

No wonder poor, silly Fergie succumbed. If someone of my spectacularly modest televisual fame keeps being assured with every postman's visit that my presence, my signature, my lentil soup recipe, my sock, for heaven's sake, would make the world of difference to this or that venture, how seductive must be the fantasy world of real big-time celebrity.

No wonder Sarah Ferguson came so quickly to believe in it herself and to trade on her pulling power. The sadness behind the folly of that comi-tragedy is that her very self-esteem became dependent on this ephemeral celebrity-esteem. Nowadays, I suspect, she finds even notoriety preferable to an existence where no one asked any longer for an interview, a photograph, or a celebrity sock.

Mind you, it's hard to see how anyone with children can ever take his or her own celebrity status seriously. My own are sublimely unaffected by having a mother who pops up from time to time on their television screen. The most I can expect is a casual 'Hi, Mum' as they zip past me on their way to the cartoons. The only time my job stirred a moment's interest was when I came home one day with a signed photograph of Cliff Richard, an enduring object of veneration to my eldest son's best friend's mother. The daughter merely sniffed and asked why I never interviewed Take That.

This benign indifference to how the parent happens to earn her crust is a good deal healthier than my own attitude as a child to my father's appearance on the television screens of the land in the guise of *Mastermind* inquisitor. Not that I was seduced by his fame. Far from it. I was paralysed by embarrassment, rendered rigid by the agony of being in the company of someone so instantly recognizable. When complete strangers called wittily as we passed, 'I've started so I'll finish, hahaha,' I curled and writhed. I took to walking several paces behind him in case someone might think we were related. I used a pretend surname at parties so that no one could say, 'Magnusson? That's an unusual name. Any relation?'

He, meanwhile, was unruffled charm itself, never appearing to mind how many times they whispered 'Pass!' as he passed, always agreeing graciously when the more sharp-eyed fans pointed out that he looked just like himself.

But me, I still curl up at the idiocies of the celebrity game. Irony of ironies that I should end up in a line of work that invites them all over again. Where's that sock?

November, 1996

133

Sweet Futility

I have decided to give up chocolate. I will be starting, er, soon. Honest.

This is a promise I have been making to myself, and to anyone who hasn't long ago giving up listening, for some time. I came closest to doing it last month on a train to Aberdeen, where I bade a sentimental farewell to a Cadbury's Boost, unwrapping it lovingly and savouring every scrummy bite as if it were my last, as I fully intended it would be.

This resolution lasted right through the day until the train home from Aberdeen, when I was ravenously hungry and nothing presented itself on the buffet trolley that would hit the spot quite as comfortably as a Cadbury's Crunchie.

The trouble is, I do seem to get more hungry, more frequently, than just about anyone I know. This has always been a source of some merriment among colleagues down the years. One, who used to refer to me as Muncher Magnusson, turned up at the hospital after the birth of my first-born bearing not flowers or bootees but several jumbo packs of Kit-Kats.

I suppose the attraction of chocolate is this marvellous combination of quelling appetite and boosting adrenaline at the same time. At school I could never face an exam without a packet of chocolate buttons placed religiously over the old ink-hole in the right-hand corner of the desk. I would award myself one at the end of each question, and two or three extra if I was stuck.

These days I find Mars Bars invaluable for getting me through long early-morning live broadcasts. There's nothing like sinking your teeth into that gooey sweetness around ten to eight, even when your co-presenter is on a rather ostentatious diet and insists on nibbling self-righteously on a mango. He won't accept my proffered bites these days anyway, ever since the morning he choked on a peanut in my Snickers. Bounty Bars are bad for that too, especially if you take a bite too near the end of the film that's going out while you're munching, and the camera returns to catch you in mid-gag. But Mars Bars are just the ticket. Thick, choco-latey, gooey and with all the glucose you need to survive another on-air encounter with Michael Fish, they slide down the throat like a dream.

I suppose I must be an addict. I can't enjoy a cup of coffee or tea without chocolate. I can't curl up with a book or write an article without a mug in one hand and a bar of something in the other. (Kit-Kat this morning. I've just polished off the last in the tin and my mind's eye is already roving round the kitchen in search of the next fix.)

Last Easter my husband was genuinely shocked to find me snaf-fling the children's eggs – not all, you understand, just a piece here and there – on the grounds, which seemed perfectly sound at the time, that too much chocolate wasn't good for them.

Well, it's not good for them, is it? It's not good for me either, but because the vast tonnage I've consumed over the years hasn't shown up much yet around the thighs, it's easy to forget. I have this recurring nightmare that one day, maybe after the menopause, all the chocolate I've ever eaten will turn to fat all at once and I'll roll off into the horizon to meet my nemesis and lament, too late, my wicked ways.

In the meantime, it would undoubtedly help if I did more exer-cise and stuck to regular mealtimes and a better diet. But, like all the marvellous lifestyle changes I fantasize about, including cycling to the paper shop, going vegetarian and remembering to walk the dog, these dreams are constantly thwarted by the lifestyle I currently enjoy. Namely, children.

I'm always entranced by those people whose breakfast routine, as recorded in columns like 'A Life in the Day', involves squeezing oranges to make their own juice, grinding coffee beans and carefully weighing out the ingredients of their organic muesli. In our house my luck is seriously in if I can grab a piece of toast on my way out of the door. Most mornings that one precious sliver of toast is either whipped from under my nose by some passing child or tenderly fed to the dog by the toddler.

Then there's teatime, a sort of lowest common denominator meal: in other words, what you're left with once you've taken into account all the food some child or other doesn't like. The bigger the family, the lower the denominator. I won't go into the sordid details here, but let's just say we do a busy line in baked beans and it's enough to drive any self-respecting parent to chocolate.

As for exercise, well, that's a laugh. Just try a brisk walk with a toddler inspecting every puddle. Or try fitting in the gym between school pick-ups, supermarket trips, dashes to the garage for antifreeze, or to the clinic for the eighteen-month health check, or to the toy shop for a present for a birthday party you've forgotten all about, or to the café to read the newspapers and remind yourself that you're supposed to be a journalist (and, of course, to nibble a wee slice of chocolate shortbread while you're doing it, because the baby dropped your toast in his Rice Krispies and you're getting a bit peckish). It's hopeless.

Mind you, there's always the exercise you get tearing up and down the stairs at least fifty times every evening, chasing children up to bed, then chasing them up again, and again, then rushing up to tell them to be quiet or they'll wake the baby, then storming up to get the baby back to sleep, then tearing down to capture an escapee who made off while you were engaged in yet another rendition of 'Little Birdie in the Sky' in the baby's room, back up with him, then down for some water, up to deliver it, down to fetch the Calpol for some sore throat or other, up with that, down to harass the next in line for bed, up to check he's in. And so on.

This certainly keeps the legs moving, but I'm not sure it's quite what the fitness gurus ordered. Anyway, any value to the constitution is of course immediately wiped out by what follows. By the time the last child is ensconced and all is more or less at peace, there's only one thing for it: a cup of tea and a biscuit. A chocolate biscuit, of course.

But I'll be stopping soon.

December, 1996

138

King Herod and King Sam

I don't know whether they are excessively literal-minded or whether I have somehow blighted their Yuletide imaginations, but my children don't believe in Santa Claus.

The rot set in around the age of four with the eldest who, after several searching questions about reindeer and the force of gravity, asked me point-blank if this Father Christmas lark were true. Now this was a difficult one, because we were also busy tackling the veracity of the Virgin Birth and those other tricky theological enquiries like 'Who made God, anyway?', which usually arrive in the middle of a noisy bath or when you're juggling an omelette. I thought I would be storing up a lot of trouble for myself if I had to bring flying men with red coats and white beards into the metaphysical equation.

Indeed this danger was confirmed only the other day by a friend who said that, on being informed at the age of nine or so that the whole thing was a fairytale, his daughter had rounded on him. 'And what other lies have you been telling me?' she snarled.

At least I avoided that one. 'The Santa story is true if you want it to be,' I equivocated that Christmas night, as my pint-sized apostate and I gazed out at the stars. 'So it's not true, then?' he persisted. 'No,' I said sadly, feeling the magic slipping away like stardust between my fingers. 'It's a great story and it's fun to believe in it, but it's not true.'

The next son, a child who likes to dream dreams and would

undoubtedly have cherished the fantasy for longer, never stood a chance. His brother took a keen pleasure in placing the facts of the matter before him at an early age, and Santa Claus quickly assumed a status similar to that of the Tooth Fairy: well worth cultivating as a source of largesse and certainly able to evoke ecstatic professions of belief when there's a chance of booty from the garden centre grotto, but never attracting the passionate conviction of the true believer.

The present five-year-old inhabits such bizarre imaginative realms of his own that the Santa Claus story is too tame to bother him either way. He is currently deeply into a personal reworking of the Mary and Joseph story, in which Herod stars as a sort of wicked Power Ranger and the ending is, to say the least, unconventional.

'And Herod wanted to die Jesus with his magic finger,' he was explaining to me last night. '"*Die!*" shouted Herod. And Jesus died and was never seen again.'

We clearly have some way to go with the theological education here. 'Actually,' I pointed out, 'it was Herod who died in the end, not Jesus.'

'Oh, I know how that happened,' said our master of fables. 'After Herod died, there was a new king called King Sam. He loved Jesus, but he hated God and the shepherds. He came with his soldiers and went "Aha", and Jesus was all right again.'

This is the child who informed me a few weeks ago that personally he wasn't too keen on God. Why not? 'Because,' he declared, with a theatrical sob, 'I wanted three legs.'

So his imagination has been far too crowded this Christmas to have much room for reindeer and sleighs. Indeed, as long as a plentiful supply of presents is guaranteed, he doesn't seem to mind how they're conveyed.

Not so his six-year-old sister. She has approached the whole Santa business with a rather touching maturity. By last year her older brothers had sowed all the usual doubts and I had done my well-rehearsed spiel about the magic being there if you wanted it to be. I think at first she rather enjoyed a sense of intellectual superiority over her benighted peers who still believed in fairytales.

But she must have felt deep-down that she was missing something, because she told me a few evenings ago that this Christmas she would be claiming the magic. 'I know it's not true really,' she said, 'but I'm going to believe in Santa Claus anyway, because I want to.' I find this willing suspension of disbelief both wise and very moving. 'Don't forget,' she whispered, as I switched the bedroom light out. 'Remember, I believe now.'

Mind you, having all these unbelievers and temporary believers in the family does tend to make the present-giving business a somewhat cold-blooded affair. We hang up the stockings all right, amid scenes of high anticipation, but someone will be sure to add, 'Remember to fill them right to the top, Dad.'

No letters to Santa for us, or wistful hopes that his elves will have this or that special gift in their store. Instead, they drink in every gross television advert and then place their orders.

My grandfather, growing up with seven siblings in a small croft far in the north of Iceland, received one orange every Christmas. That was it. This orange was longed for and looked forward to; it was gazed at and stroked and treasured and savoured, nibble by nibble, for hours.

His great-grandson, on the other hand, has just asked if I would supply him with an Argos catalogue so that he can make his selection in comfort. There is certainly scope for dreams in the Argos catalogue, but it's not, I told him, what Christmas should be about. We're talking wonder here, I lectured, anticipation, hope, surprise, not coolly marking up a catalogue. I recounted in lyrical terms the story of the Christmas orange on the frosty hillside croft in Akureyri.

He listened patiently and said Curry's would do just as well. 'I was just trying to make it easier for you, Mum,' he sighed. He later presented me with a Curry's catalogue that had fallen out of the Sunday papers. 'Perhaps,' he suggested, with a dead-pan gleam, 'Santa Claus would be interested in the item I've marked with an asterisk on page seven.'

December, 1996

Merry Christmas, Wall

Maybe it was because my sister's children were confined to barracks with, as she explained theatrically on the phone, 'foot and mouth disease. It's horrible. They've all got it.' Maybe it was that most of mine are at last approaching the age of civilization, and the toddler was so overwhelmed with the attention of fawning adults that he had nothing to complain about. Whatever the reason, my mother pronounced this a historic Christmas.

'It's the first I can remember for years that nobody whinged,' she sighed happily.

'That's because we had all the whingeing down here,' muttered my sister grimly in a later phone call from her London outpost, evoking a ghastly picture of mouth ulcers, tantrums and pints of Calpol poured down three screaming maws. 'But I do hope you all enjoyed your turkey,' she added sweetly.

I'm afraid we did. Even the dire news from the south and the prospect of missing what promised to have been the evening's star cabaret performance – my four-year-old nephew doing his spirited rendition from the school nativity, 'Rock around the Flock' – was not enough to mar the proceedings. For once Christmas was civilized, it was rather beautiful, it was (to use a word almost foreign to our household) serene.

We do things the Icelandic way. The festivities begin at six o'clock sharp on Christmas Eve, when the family rolls up, dressed to the nines, and we gather round the fire to sing carols and try to remember the words of the Icelandic ones which my grand-parents used to sing in the days when the whole clan assembled at their house in Edinburgh and gasped in wonder at the huge tree with real flickering candles, which was my grandfather's pride and joy.

I'm biased, of course, because I've never known it any other way, but I've always thought that celebrating through the evening, rather than during the next day, gives Christmas a specially magical flavour. It's the contrast between the darkness and the bitter cold outside, enhanced occasionally by snow (in fact, one son went round spraying the windows with fake white this time and even the illusion was bewitching), and all the light and sparkle within.

The turkey, which I had nursed as fastidiously all day as my poor sister her foot and mouth victims, emerged to my genuine amaze-ment looking and tasting more or less as it was supposed to, although I have a feeling I may have stuffed the wrong aper-ture. 'Are you quite sure that's its bottom, Mum?' one child had enquired suspiciously, as I gaily rammed sausages in. I wasn't entirely sure, but when you've spent one memorable Christmas Eve a few years back quick-frying turkey fillets because you forgot to switch the oven on, anatomical niceties are a small matter indeed.

Actually the real triumph of the meal was the Icelandic dishes which another sister had gone to infinite trouble to produce so that our father could enjoy for the first time in decades the genuine tastes of his own childhood Christmases. We started with *hrísgrjóna-grautur*, a sort of rice pudding eaten with cinnamon and milk; it seemed bizarre as starters go, but my father lapped it up with a dreamy smile. And at the end there was a feather-light lemon mousse, which is the only dessert I have seen him eat in my entire life. In between, he carved the turkey and told his Christmas joke, which we all pretended never to have heard before, and beamed beatifically throughout. As ever, the best gifts are the ones you give to other people.

Or maybe, in some cases, the ones you receive. Certainly, the recycled variety proved a great hit when we moved on to the next highlight of the evening, the opening of the presents round the tree. I was admiring a neat little Fisher Price camera which one son had just opened. 'That's nice, but I'm sure we've got one already,' I whispered, hoping the giver would be none the wiser. 'We do,' said the son. 'That's it.'

All round the room there were gasps of exaggerated thanks and praise as ancient bits of railway track and broken necklaces emerged from large, ostentatiously wrapped parcels. 'I'm over-whelmed,' muttered my brother, studying a wooden train station.

The chief giver of these gifts danced around with his shirt hanging out and his kilt back to front, in an ecstasy of delight. He had apparently recovered from the symptoms which he described to me earlier as 'a poisoned sound inside my chest and a dead tummy', which I took to be a combination of excitement and chocolate. This was his moment, and he had been waiting for it since before six o'clock when we overheard him wandering down the stairs, observing happily, 'Merry Christmas, carpet. Merry Christmas, banister. Merry Christmas, wall.'

His elder sister had also gone in for home-prepared presents in a big way, with gift tags inscribed with messages such as 'To Dad, Sorry for all the rong things I have don' and 'To Grandma, I think of you all the time'. My mother studied her present, a tube containing six grains of rice, three pasta shells, a dice and a safety pin, for some time before giving up and asking for elucidation. 'It's a shaker, Grandma. You just shake it. See?' Ah. She saw.

It was a happy time. Like many families, we have known less happy Christmases, and the sadness of being without the one we can never have back still has the capacity to pierce our most joyful moments to the heart. But, as I put the lights out on our Christmas Eve, and thought about the Dunblane families and all the others for whom loss is still fresh and raw and angry, I realized that joy, though it may take years and years, can creep up on you all the same.

December, 1996

145

PART THREE

PART THREE

Of Roses and Cabbages

I've tried to keep my husband out of these pages as much as possible. A chap has his dignity after all, and marriage is a tricky enough business without my having to explain why the lady in the newsagent's knows the colour of his boxer-shorts. Having said that, he is not entirely averse to a spot of notoriety now and again, since this is a man for whom the word self-assurance might have been coined.

While I remain terminally undecided and gloom-ridden in the face of life's more important choices, he has the advantage of always knowing with sunny certainty that he is right. I suppose if this hadn't been so, we might never have got hitched in the first place. I was so paralysed with indecision about whether to marry him that he more or less had to order me to get on with it.

The proposal had gone fine. We were celebrating our joint birthday in a romantic London dockside restaurant, struggling to hear ourselves speak above the babble of excited Japanese tourists at the next table, when he suddenly lobbed the how-about-it question and sat back, clearly expecting me to request a few years to think about it. Instead, I stunned us both by saying yes. Immediately. Just like that. Without a second's hesitation.

Naturally I regretted it within hours. Before we even had the chance to mention it to anyone, I was already suggesting that we might keep quiet about all this until I had given it a bit more thought. I mean, lifelong commitment seemed too momentous a thing to accede to impulsively in a rosy glow of wine with the sun setting on the Thames. Nonsense, said he. My deepest instincts had spoken and he was going to tell the whole world. Maddeningly confident that mature reflection would lead any woman to conclude she was better off with him than without, he made it clear that he expected to see me at the altar and left me to wallow in my angst.

By the time the wedding was a mere month or two distant, I was in such a state – agonizing over whether I had the temperament to give up my independence, worrying (since I only wanted to do this thing once) that the possible fifty years or so ahead of us seemed an awful long time – that I started coming out in spots. There were spots everywhere, big red angry things like a nettle rash all over but concentrating with particular venom on my bottom, prompting an uncle of my beloved's to remark, acidly *sotto voce*, 'Has that girl of yours got ants in her pants?', which was more accurate than he knew.

In the end, it was my mother who landed me in it. A long letter arrived from her one day, typed in the fast, slightly hit-or-miss, one-fingered style she had perfected as a newspaper reporter. She understood that my doubts were less over my feelings than over whether I possessed the capacity, or even the desire, to give up the even tenor of my self-centred ways for, as she put it, 'paths unknown, depths unplumbed, a future directed by considerations other than your own comfort, ambition, peace of mind, or even just the whims of the moment.'

She suggested that I see marriage as a new adventure with the spice of danger, and she helped me to understand how a couple could live together in harmony without sacrificing their selfhood.

'You don't give up your independence by thinking of the other person first,' she wrote. 'Because *you* make the decision to give, you are not having anything taken away from you. You are not surrendering your personality, you're adding to it. Since he is doing the same on your behalf' (here's hoping, I thought) 'no one feels put upon. Of course there are off-days, tired days, spotty days, but love and a sense of humour will get you by.'

150

Mindful of how I was baulking at the prospect of being shackled for the next half-century, she pointed out that commitment was a one day at a time business. 'In fact,' she said, 'if you could just promise to love, honour and cherish for a day at a time, and renew your vow in your own mind every morning, it would all add up to "till death us do part".'

Sure, she said, you could put it off – commitment, marriage, family, the lot. 'You could keep putting it off. You could opt out altogether from this most challenging of all realms of living, with its heights of joy, depths of despair, its demands on resources of character and personality hardly suspected and maybe never needed in any other walk of life. Many people get through life without taking this step. Many would have loved to do it and never got the chance.'

But in turning away from it, she implied, I would be missing out on something rather difficult, but uniquely precious. It was wise advice from a woman who knew all about the strains that throwing your lot in with family life can bring, not least the pain of loss. The fourth of her five children, the beloved son who had bewitched her heart after a run of three daughters, died in a road accident a few days before his twelfth birthday. Her wisdom was hard won.

But she was right. Marriage and family life are difficult and exhilarating in about equal measure. Most of us, I suspect, will attest that rubbing along in close quarters with partner and strong-minded children does indeed demand 'resources of character' with which I, for one, am spectacularly poorly equipped by nature: tolerance, patience and an endless capacity to give and take, or more usually give and give. The reward, if you can look at it in these terms, is the times of piercing happiness, of camaraderie, of fulfilment beyond anything even the most satisfying professional life has to offer.

H. L. Mencken defined an idealist as a man who, on noticing that a rose smells better than a cabbage, assumes it will also make better soup. I'm the last person to suggest that family life, although wonderfully fragrant at times, necessarily makes good soup. Relationships can sour it, tragedy can drain its goodness and maturing children are unpredictable ingredients. But you don't need to be an idealist to contend that sometimes, at its best, there is nothing to beat the taste.

For children, too, the experience of growing up in a family is a useful training for life. Survival depends on getting along with siblings who have vastly different personalities, learning to wait your turn and being prepared to share the state-of-the-art Nintendo game you've just spent your savings on. My brood has also had to learn to rub along with a succession of au pairs of varying susceptibilities and a busy traffic in visitors. They long ago became used to greeting strangers in the kitchen of a morning as if they'd known them all their life.

We get a lot of visitors, although you may wonder why, since they come in the full knowledge that what awaits them here is a road that will wreak havoc with their car suspension, meals they may end up cooking themselves, early-morning goosing by the dog and general bedlam.

One friend of sane mind and his own volition even chose to stay with us for a year. He was homeless at the time, which may have had something to do with it – or at least he was during the week, when his new job at Glasgow University kept him away from his home in Aberdeen. Even the mile-long trek to the village bus-stop every morning, invariably followed by the dog which meant turning back, manhandling her into the house, starting again and missing the bus, proved more attractive than commuting from north-east Scotland.

And so he became our lodger. He escaped the early-morning attentions of the hound, who has only recently discovered how to open the door of the spare room and now greets sleeping guests by burrowing under the bottom of the duvet and nuzzling their nether regions in a friendly fashion. But he did have to cope with a degree of uncertainty about whom else he might find in his bed of an evening, especially when he had been away for the weekend and supplanted by other guests. After discovering two elderly ladies in his bed one night, he resorted to inching the door open each evening and tip-toeing into the room in a very gingerly manner.

Unassuming to the point of bringing home his own Chinese carry-outs for supper, he proved a most welcome asset to the household, and the long debates about Scottish devolution over a bottle of Laphroaig at the kitchen table certainly raised the tone of the household's late-night conversation beyond the usual scrap over whose turn it might be to load the dishwasher.

Another long-term guest was Colin the film-editor, who set up a dazzling bank of computers in the study and spent many happy weeks cutting a television drama by day and educating the children in the finer points of Nintendo play by night. He had long red hair tied back in a pony-tail and wore shirts emblazoned with Disney characters. The children adored him.

Then there are the visitors from abroad. One of the things we were never warned about au pairs is that they too have guests, and the ones we've picked precisely because they come from large families and will feel at home with ours, are likely to have larger than average quantities of visitors. Nezia, the Dutch girl, was a case in point. She announced one day that her mother and father would be visiting from Holland. When I enquired, aghast, about the arrangements she had in mind for them, she said airily that they wouldn't need a room. I imagined bed and breakfast in the next town.

A few weeks later I was looking idly out of the window when I spotted an enormous vehicle trundling along the farm track towards the house. Bit early for the binmen, I thought. The vehicle thundered on, revealing itself, as it rounded the lawn and parked by the side of the house, to be a vast mobile home which owed its slightly ramshackle appearance to the fact that the Dutch parents had constructed it themselves from odd wheels and bits of van. It seemed to suit them splendidly, however. They settled down cheerfully to life in the garden, popping into the house from time to time to have showers and mend things.

It really is most touching, this impulse that guests have to help us out. Nezia's father didn't speak much English but he knew a fuse-box when he saw one and was soon pottering around doing all the long-neglected household jobs that are too embarrassingly small to call in an expert for but quite beyond the competence of the hand-less pair who run this household.

He even spent a morning picking rubble, stone by stone, out of a long patch of earth so that my daughter, who had expressed a sudden interest in horticulture, could plant cabbages in it. She had never knowingly eaten a cabbage in her life. 'Please don't go to all that trouble', we said, knowing perfectly well she would plant half a packet of seeds and never look at it again. 'No, no,' he insisted with Teutonic zeal. 'I do it. I do it.' He did it, too, and we never did see any cabbages.

They were delightful people and we waved goodbye with fond pleas to come again any time. They didn't, but the mobile home did. Later that summer it rolled up again and disgorged Nezia's brother, sister-in-law and six children. In fact, I seem to recall there were nine of them, so maybe there were seven children. All I know is that I returned from a trip to the Western Isles to find the Greenham Common peace camp installed at the side of the house, with towels and knickers stretched on a line behind assorted tents, and a bonfire burning playfully in the middle of the grass. The mobile home was parked in the usual place. My husband said not to worry, the two sets of children had been getting on very well together across the language barrier and this was as good a way as any of occupying them in the school holidays.

Nevertheless it was some relief that they left before his own parents made one of their periodic visits from their home in Hartlepool. They put up with a lot here, but twelve children might just have tipped them over the edge.

My father-in-law is another of those kindly types sent to us from above who likes to keep busy around the house. Painting is his forte, especially doors and windowsills. 'Just get me a pot of white gloss in B&Q on your way past,' he'll say on the second day, 'and I'll get started on them doors.' Our hearts leap. My mother-in-law also has a knack of uttering those words you long to hear people saying like 'Pass that dish-towel, will you, and I'll just get these plates out of the way.'

The children take all the coming and going in their stride.

Extended family, mother's helps, lodgers, far-travelled friends and every hapless caller from the man reading the electricity meter who's stayed for a cup of tea, to the minister and his dog, the girl doing my husband's typing, the neighbour who's volunteered to rejuvenate our vegetable patch with the novel strategy of growing vegetables in it and the farmer on his way through to catch a cow in the back garden . . . all in all, it's a motley crew we have around the place here. Of course I like to think it helps the children to acquire a few of the social skills they will need to make their way in the world. I fear it's more likely to turn them into recluses.

Maybe the babbling Japanese tourists at St Katherine's Dock were an omen, after all, for the House of Babel we would one day create together. 'And what's more,' puts in my husband, 'just remember I was right.'

Dinner for Three

Last week we took our daughter out to dinner to celebrate her seventh birthday. Just her. 'When did we three last do something together without the others?' I mused on the way to the restaurant. 'The day I was born?' she ventured, after much thought. She was probably right.

That's the way things go in big families. The eldest enjoys a halcyon year or two of single-minded devotion at the beginning, and the youngest has his favoured time at the other end. But for those in between there is always someone else around: a baby whingeing in a buggy; a younger brother to demand that if there are any treats going, he comes along too; an older sister who invariably gets to stay up later, however old you are. Always a clutch of others with their own demands, tastes and hard-won rights to interfere with your own.

'It's not fair,' echoes round our house at least a hundred times a day. Have children always had such a keen sense of fairness, such an eagle eye for the slightest teetering of the scales of justice in another's favour? (The most exaggerated plunge of the scales in the right direction will, naturally, be overlooked.) Or is it all part of growing up in a society where children are both seen and constantly, interminably, heard?

No down-trodden worker or persecuted innocent fights for his rights with more tenacity, for instance, than a five-year-old who doesn't see why a mere accident of birth should have consigned him to what feels like an eternity of going to bed before three of his siblings. However many birthdays he notches up, they always manage to sneak in a few of their own, thus entrenching their status in the bedtime hierarchy. Only the mollifying observation that one final sibling continues to be despatched to slumber before him is holding this powerful grievance in check.

Since I can think of no other way of managing the bedtime business without the whole thing sliding into anarchy, he's fighting a losing battle here. But the anguished cries of 'Why, Mum? Why is it always me? It's not fair!' as he's hauled away in the tumbril, make me feel like some heartless despot at the head of a corrupt regime of rank and privilege.

Why him, indeed? Because he was born fourth. Because I have to operate a system, and if I move him up the queue you'll hear the cries of 'It's not fair' from numbers three, two and one on the other side of the Irish Sea. But the *ancien régime*, I fear, is tottering under the weight of reason. If the toddler turns out to be an argumentative type, we're in for revolution.

But thank heavens for birthdays. Everyone accepts that they are occasions of unique privilege, and the exclusive dinner when they reach an age to appreciate it has proved a winner. The daughter was quite dizzy at the novelty of choosing where to sit without having to elbow a brother or four out of the way, trying out some of her self-made jokes without the usual roars of derision, helping herself to whacking great dollops of mint sauce without provoking outrage up and down the table from her rivals in greed, and for three whole hours effortlessly commanding her parents' attention without being told to let someone else have a say.

We first tried this *dîner à trois* four years ago when the eldest turned seven. We took him to an extremely posh mansion-turned-hotel in Buckinghamshire called Cliveden House, where Nancy Astor once lived, Profumo and Keeler dallied in the swimming pool and Emma Thompson married Kenneth Branagh in a ceremony of such bizarre extravagance that it had the eyes of all us locals popping. It was only a mile or two from where we lived, and we had long hungered for an excuse to size up the high life inside.

After all, this birthday business is as much an indulgence for parents as child.

The son entered fully into the spirit of the occasion and insisted on wearing one of his birthday presents – a black plastic magician's top hat, out of which he had earlier conjured a cardboard rabbit and a couple of doves. It was a sartorial touch which he felt would do justice to the grandeur of the occasion. He too had stomped around the National Trust-owned grounds of Cliveden of a Saturday afternoon, peering through the tall windows and wondering at the chandeliers and the huge oil paintings of ladies with foot-high hair-dos. A certain aristocratic hauteur in the wardrobe was called for, he felt. He looked like a midget Fat Controller.

After crunching along a Daimler-littered driveway and handing over the keys of our beaten-up Spacewagon, we were greeted by a footman who gravely collected our coats and without the merest twitch of an eyebrow, without the most fleeting ghost of a smile, asked if Sir would like to give him his hat. Sir handed it over graciously and was gratified to see it placed prominently on a rack of its own.

The house had big fireplaces crackling with flame, sumptuous wood panelling and quite the most breathtakingly perfect Christmas tree any of us had ever seen. The food was good, too. And the company was entrancing. What delightful creatures children would be if they behaved like that all the time. Such manners. Such repartee. By which I mean he remembered to use his knife and we laughed a lot.

The second son passed up his chance of a civilized birthday night out with the aged parents in favour of annihilating his friends with a laser gun at one of those ghastly zapping places, but the daughter leaped at it when her turn came. We had to do without the mansion and footman this time, but a menu of stewed monkfish tails and wild pheasant was quite exotic enough for her. She announced pleasantly that she didn't fancy anything and would probably starve.

In fact, she ended up tucking into roast rack of lamb with gusto, and was less than convincing when she observed, as the waiter approached to see if she would like anything else, that she would just have some beans and toast when she got home, thank you.

I fear this one may lack the aristocratic touch.

January, 1997

Real Superwomen

Let's get this straight. Nicola Horlick, the mother of five whose sensational resignation from her high-powered job in a merchant bank entertained us all vastly for a few days, undoubtedly has many qualities. But she is no superwoman.

Possibly she wouldn't claim to be. I notice it is others who have been quick to garland her with the superwoman soubriquet and, since she has been struggling for years with a desperately sick child along with everything else, I suspect her life is less dauntingly efficient than it appears.

But nobody with a secretary to answer phones and letters, two domestic helpers a day to cook, clean, wash clothes and iron, and a full-time nanny for the children needs many special skills beyond being good at her job, a flair for organizing staff and the ability to sink into a chair at the end of the day and say 'Come to Mummy, darlings.'

The fact is, it's a fallacy that the more children and the more demanding the job, the more of a superwoman the mother must be to manage it all. The truth is that once you start paying someone else to do everything except actually have the babies, it's not very difficult at all.

I know plenty of real superwomen. They're the ones who spend two hours trailing a wailing toddler and a fractious three-year-old all the way to the supermarket and back for the one item they forgot when they did the same thing yesterday, and who do it without losing their temper.

They're the ones who teach other people's children all day, then go home to make the tea, mark the jotters, supervise their own children's homework, turn out for the football club, put the kids to bed and prepare for tomorrow's class.

They're the ones who run up a costume for the school concert with one child on their knee, another under their feet and a husband asking why nobody has fed the dog.

They're the ones who would like nothing better once in a while than to get up in the morning, bid a cheerful goodbye to the children as they breakfast with the nanny and head off to do a spot of investment fund managing. Stress? You tell me anything as stressful as trying to get a howling two-year-old into his coat while ordering another for the fifth time to brush his teeth and another to try looking for his shoe down the toilet because that's where the baby put it last time.

I do have some help these days, and while my doughty au pair is not exactly staff on the Nicola Horlick scale, that support makes all the difference. It is the sheerest luxury to sit here toying with this word or that on the computer while she shivers her way round the garden, enthusing manfully over every blade of grass, every minuscule puddle that the toddler sees fit to inspect.

Since I find it infinitely easier to present television programmes than manage the ironing competently, I'm lucky to be able to do the one in order to avoid the other. So when people hear how many children I have, reel back in a sort of horrified admiration and stutter, 'But how on earth do you manage everything?' the answer is actually quite simple: I don't.

The hardest times were when I had fewer children and no help. I have never known days which felt so long as in the months after my first child was born. Having embarked on motherhood with the quaint notion that babies spent most of the time sleeping and the rest gurgling contentedly while you whisked round with the hoover and then got down to a good book, the birth of a child who simply cried unless he was being nursed, carried or shoogled was a terrible shock.

I used to bump him round the village in his pram for hours on end, day after day. I knew every gravestone in the churchyard off by heart; the big decision of the morning would be whether to go round the path clockwise or anti-clockwise. We visited ducks that the baby was not remotely interested in. We wandered past the village hall and I wondered how old he would have to be for us to qualify for the mother and toddler group, the acme of my social aspiration.

OK, so I was no superwoman in the Nicola Horlick sense, but I do know these early months and years dug into reserves of patience, stamina and imagination that I had never had to tap before.

It was easier when the second one came along, because I knew what I was doing and at least had a two-year-old for company. But I still contend that no investment manager in the hurly-burly of a stimulating job has it remotely as tough as the mother of two grizzly under-threes facing the long hours between lunch and teatime. What will it be today? you ask yourself after clearing up the devastated table and wiping Heinz apricot dessert off the wall. Swing-park? Shops? Phone up friend and hope she invites you to visit? Go for a drive on some pretext you can figure out later?

The friend's not in, a drive will send the children to sleep at the wrong end of the day, you can't think of a single thing you need at the shops, so you choose the swings. Getting them ready to go out takes half an hour, a couple of tantrums and a dirty nappy – which means you have to start all over again just when you've finally zipped the snow-suit up and enticed the gloves on with the help of a biscuit that's now plastered all over his face. It uses up your entire stock of patience, which in my case has never been large.

You push them the half-mile to the swing-park in the double buggy – and there should be a superwoman award for this achievement alone – straining a muscle in your arm as you try to control the side that's got the thumping great two-year-old in it to stop all three of you careering into the gutter. And at the park you nearly pull a muscle in the other arm, trying to push two swings at the same time.

And then you look at them, squealing with delight, their faces ruddy and their eyes bright, and you think there is nowhere else in the world you would rather be, and it's all worth it, and you don't care that the biggest decision you'll have made today is whether to have eggy soldiers or Dairylea sandwiches for tea. This is it. This is life.

And that was, indeed, a very special time. The current toddler has scarcely seen a swing-park and it's a loss for us both. But make no mistake. Those were the days when superwomanly qualities were required by the sackload. But no one ever said then, 'How do you do it?'

January, 1997

164

Bravehearts

The other day my daughter was telling me about William Wallace. 'He fought for Scotland,' she explained. 'Then he got chopped up by the Germans.'

She and her brothers have been on a sharp learning curve (possibly, in her case, not quite sharp enough) since we moved back to Scotland a couple of years ago: new accents, new vocabulary, new heroes, new history.

Almost as soon as we arrived, words from my childhood came bursting through the door. 'Jobby' was among the first. One son had heard it at school and been rash enough to ask what it meant. The howls of laughter, he reported, were deafening, but his delight at this wonderful new addition to the toilet lexicon over-rode the humiliation, and jobby has assumed an esteemed position among the poos, willies, piddles and pees that make conversation in our house such an elevating experience.

In fact, I regret to say that the youngest, a strong, silent type who is steaming towards his second birthday with a vocabulary consisting exclusively of 'more', 'woof', 'tractor' and 'fish', has just added a fifth word, after much painstaking tutoring by his five-year-old brother. So rare is it for this child to come up with any recognizable word at all, that we are currently being treated to the glorious spectacle of his grandmother, a woman of virginal linguistic purity, crouching on the carpet and cajoling, *sotto voce*, 'Come on now, say "bum" for Grandma.'

'Jotter' was another new word on my little Englanders. I'm not sure whether its use is confined to Scotland, but we certainly never heard it in the south-east, where dull exercise books ruled. As did the terribly boring 'P.E.' It took me years down south to get used to kitting the children out for P.E. rather than gym, and I had a delicious sense of homecoming soon after we moved here when one of them first shouted, 'I can't find my gym shoes.'

It wasn't until I heard them chattering about the school janny and the class klype, pleading for a wee shot on the computer, complaining about a sore pinkie or a jaggy throat, that I realized how long it was since I had heard these words. Call me biased, but caretaker, tell-tale, short turn, little finger and painful-in-a-sharp-kind-of-way are pallid by comparison.

Vocabulary changes a lot more quickly than accent, of course, as one son found last summer on the day England beat Scotland in the European Cup. 'Are you English?' menaced a passing youth who had heard him talking. Too frightened to open his mouth again, he pointed wordlessly to the Scotland strip he was wearing under his jacket. 'Good on you, son,' said his tormentor, and strutted off.

The older children are genuinely puzzled by this undercurrent of anti-English hostility. Only in that one incident, on a particularly emotional day, has it been directed at them personally, except in good-natured playground banter. But they pick up the vibes. 'Why do Scottish people think everything English is bad?' one of them asked recently.

I launched into a long explanation about Scotland being a small nation with a big neighbour whose regrettable tendency to invade, dominate and then periodically forget we exist had made us all a bit touchy about the English. It had given us a chip on the shoulder the size of the Wallace Monument but, he should understand, it was nothing personal.

'But all that's history,' he replied. 'Why do Scots still go on and on about the English?'

'Because it's hard to escape your history, especially when you simplify it into goodies and baddies,' I said, thinking suddenly of

166

Northern Ireland and feeling rather ashamed of the enthusiasm with which I had shown him the video of that seductive travesty, *Braveheart*.

He shrugged. 'I suppose it's just because England keeps beating you at football,' was his last word on the subject.

Whatever way you look at it, it can only be a good idea for more Scottish history to be on the syllabus, although the famous jibe that Scotland is the only country that doesn't teach its own history in its schools is a bit hard on the primaries, which seem to be rather good at it on a simple level. Certainly my children had not been here long before they were hearing about Bonnie Prince Charlie, Culloden, the Clearances, Robert the Bruce and William Wallace. Even the school pantomime this year is designed to teach them about the effects on a Scottish community of the 1872 Education (Scotland) Act.

They've also been well saturated with Robert Burns. There was nothing in their English primary to match the way in which every January the whole school here sets about learning the bard's poems by heart. Since my lot have all learned each other's verses, by dint of hearing them repeated ad infinitum on the way to school, they now have several off by heart. It certainly added spice to the normal back-seat bedlam to have one getting noisily fou and unco' happy while another was trilling on about birds chittering in the thorn and a third telling them both to shut up because he needed to get into the mood for John Anderson, my jo.

This has been a great education for me, too, since I never got round to learning anything by Burns at school and am now reciting the stuff in my dreams. I've scurried off to *The Concise Scots Dictionary* to look up 'skellum' and 'blellum'; I've led discourses on the phonetic differences between 'sairly' and 'sorely', 'lang' and 'long'; I've boned up on eighteenth-century farming; I've waxed lyrical about how you don't need exotic experience to be a good writer – a louse crawling up a hat will do fine.

It's all been great fun, and a considerable improvement on learning how to do long division all over again in a bizarre new way, which was my chief homework nightmare last term.

Meanwhile, I still have a little educating to do on sporting matters. Half of the clan have become avid supporters of Scotland (in fact, even in England the son with the Scottish football strip was susceptible to maternal pressure on this matter), while the other half, under the tyrannical influence of their Hartlepool-born father, continue to cheer for the wrong side. Time to show *Braveheart* again, perhaps?

February, 1997

Breakfast Tales

I've had many a welcome birthday present in my time, but none received with such fervent whoops of exultation and gratitude as the message tucked inside my sister's card back in October. It said, and the words are engraved on my heart: 'This entitles the bearers to one day and one night without children at a time of their choosing.' Last weekend we claimed it.

Having long ago made our peace with the fact that holidays *en grande famille* may be fun – they may even, to stretch a point, be enjoyable – but they leave you considerably more whacked than before you started, we have honed to a fine art the twenty-four-hour adults-only break. This entails packing two weeks' worth of languid self-pampering into one day. Any less than that, and you don't have time to unwind; any more, and your babysitters are calling for the men in white coats.

So we headed for a little bolt-hole of luxury we've discovered only forty minutes' drive from our front door, all log fires and low ceilings and rushing burn and tall, bare trees scratching the sky, although for some unaccountable reason the proprietors have now painted the beautiful old walls the shade of one of Barbara Cartland's more violently cerise lipsticks and stopped giving you big starched napkins with your breakfast. These details matter in paradise.

The chief luxury of these breaks is rediscovering the many less celebrated pleasures of the double bed. Like the long untasted joy of waking up with your head still on the pillow, instead of arched at ninety degrees to accommodate the row of heads that have materialized in the course of the night. Or the delicious indulgence of spending the entire night actually *in* the bed, as opposed to draped perilously along the edge. Or the quiet ecstasy of sleeping without a small but lethal foot thumping grumpily against your midriff. Oh yes, we know how to live.

And there's more. There's breakfast. Forgive me if I rave, but unless you've spent what sometimes seems like a lifetime of breakfasts picking toast out of your tea and Rice Krispies off the floor, arbitrating furious arguments over who gets some ridiculous plastic bauble from the Coco-Pop box and never managing more than a bite of cold toast yourself, you may not fully grasp the heady delight of sitting quietly in bed, sipping coffee with nothing floating in it and serenely piercing a perfectly poached egg while your beloved regales you with stories about his grandfather.

The excitement's killing, I hear you say. But you have to understand that talking to each other, and the even more reckless pleasure of concentrating on the answers, are another of these twenty-four-hour luxuries. By the end of dinner the night before, we had strolled through the basics: the leaky dishwasher, the problem with the fridge door, the latest witticism from the five-year-old and the heart-stopping size of the central heating bill.

But by morning we had moved on to those rarefied conversational heights that we normally only glimpse from the foothills of married life, tantalizingly out of reach beyond the din of the children, beyond the snatched consultations about whose job it is to pay the milkman, or how a shirt that last night was languishing behind the bathroom door can possibly be washed, ironed and waiting breathlessly in the cupboard by morning, or what the chances are of the Christmas tree finding its way from outside the front door to the rubbish dump by Easter.

For the other sort of conversation you need time, peace and a long enough disengagement from practical affairs to be able to say, 'No, do tell me,' when your partner suddenly stops forking sausage and fried tomato into his mouth, gazes dreamily into the middle distance and asks if he's ever told you about his ancestral line.

Thus it is that I am able to report that his grandfather was an under-age infantryman in the Boer War and a conscientious objector in the First World War, a rag-and-bone man by trade (although, as my husband pointed out primly, he managed to get others to do the actual collecting) who became the untutored minister of a tiny Nonconformist church in the north-east of England.

When the call to the trenches came, he offered to go as a stretcher-bearer but claimed his right as a minister not to take up arms. The recruiting officer didn't believe his Nonconformist credentials and promptly locked him up in Wormwood Scrubs, far to the south, pending an enquiry. His wife and children were left behind with nothing.

While awaiting His Majesty's pleasure in London, he hob-nobbed with university professors and other erudite conscientious objectors, and by the time the authorities let him go with an apology six months later, he had become quite a scholar in Greek and Hebrew. But the strain of it all had told and his hair was now completely white. His wife didn't recognize him.

And then the pathetic footnote that nearly had me snuffling into the marmalade. He hadn't been home long before he discovered a cache of money behind the clock on the mantelpiece, which he was told had been pushed under the door every few weeks by some anonymous hand. Clearly it was some kindly benefactor, but his wife had been so terrified of the authorities who had incarcerated her husband for reasons she didn't understand, that she thought it was a trap. Some days her children barely ate, but she never dared to touch that money. They never found out who had left it.

And that concluded the grandfather's tale. The coffee was cold but my husband was just hotting up. We were well into his father's exploits in the Normandy landings, and I was preparing to let fly with my uncle's escape from an Italian prison-of-war camp, when reception rang to say we were supposed to be out of the room an hour ago.

Twenty-four hours of peace and a hundred years of history. I can thoroughly recommend it.

February, 1997

172

Embarrassment

He left the cinema with his arms glued awkwardly to his sides, his shoulders hunched, his head bowed implacably towards his big, black boots and his eyes darting in alarm from side to side. He had been hit by a social crisis of mammoth proportions: spotted by two of his friends in a public place *with his father.*

In the middle of an animated discussion about the filmic merits of the new sci-fi spoof, *Mars Attack*, he suddenly froze and then metamorphosed instantly into an alien himself. We know this creature by now. It appears with unfailing regularity whenever peers and parents, by some desperate mischance, fetch up in the same social scenario, and it sticks around until all danger is completely past, by which I mean the danger of the parent doing something inexpressibly embarrassing, like speaking.

Once the bowed head and clenched fists have signalled to the parent that a hearty 'Hello boys. Enjoy the film?' is simply not tolerable, and the said parent has picked up the message and acted as if he too has never seen these boys in his life before, the clouds will clear, the shoulders relax, the head rise by degrees and the amiable child you were talking to a moment ago will be back. If by any chance, however, the dense parent has missed the signals and acknowledged the friends' existence with perhaps a cheery nod or, horror of horrors, a friendly word, the process may take longer and is likely to involve passionate recriminations of the 'Why do you always have to do this to me?' sort.

For my part, I do try not to embarrass him more than is entirely necessary because I can remember all too keenly having to insist that my own mother rallied the school hockey team from behind a hedge rather than on the sideline, where everyone could see she belonged to me. She didn't fare much better with my sister either, who in the middle of one match felt constrained to send her right-winger across with an urgent request. 'Mrs Magnusson,' whispered the messenger politely, 'Margaret says will you please shut up.'

But sometimes you do forget. 'Mum,' said my eldest the other week, as he rubbed hair-dye out of his ear after the school panto-mime, 'why did you shout out in the middle of the performance?'

'Wasn't the audience supposed to join in at that point?'

'Yes,' he conceded. 'Yes, they were. But why did it have to be you?'

Ah, why indeed? Because I thought I was helping, because I was entering into the spirit of the thing, because I forgot the cardinal rule of this pre-teen stage of parenthood, which is never, but never, to draw attention to yourself in any way, at any time, in any place outside the home, and even there be careful if he's got friends around.

'So you realized it was me, did you?' I asked.

'Of course I did. Everyone else on the stage looked straight at me. It was so embarrassing.'

Since I was watching at the time with the eagle-eyed attention that mothers devote to any stage that contains their offspring, I can personally attest that nobody's eyes so much as flickered in his direction. But no. Nothing would convince him that every eye in the hall was not pinned accusingly on him with the awful, wordless charge: 'Your mother spoke.'

Mind you, he wasn't alone in his discomfiture. One of the fathers behind me in the audience also shouted an answer, and from low on the seat next to him, getting lower all the time, a little voice pleaded despairingly, 'Oh Daddy, please. . .'

So when does it happen, this transition from children who embarrass their parents by asking in loud interested tones why that man has got such an ugly face or announcing in the reverent hush that anticipates the choir's first note that there's a poo on the way, to parents who find themselves cast unawares in the same role themselves?

Since I am regularly invited to upbraid, lambast and, if I could possibly see my way to biffing, a spot of that too, any playmate of my five-year-old's whom he feels has stepped out of line, the parent–peer traumatic syndrome has certainly not set in at that age. At seven, my daughter would prefer me not to do or say anything too *loud* in public, but she can at least still tolerate my presence and even a kiss outside the school gate.

Beyond eight, though, things start to get difficult. Even saying goodbye is just a fraction too close to the bone. The older boys, who remain at home the soppiest, slobberiest, most affectionate characters on earth, start to stiffen as soon as the school hoves into view. The best strategy for getting them out of the car pronto is to murmur innocently, 'How about a kiss before you go, then?'

Indeed the only thing that will currently embarrass the eldest more than a cheery 'Goodbye, love' in a public space within a mile of the school is to open the car door while the tape of 'The Smurfs' is still playing for the younger ones. Although he's the one who bought it in the first place, that was last year and it is now so uncool as to be positively tropical. He starts checking that the windows are closed and begging for the volume to be reduced when the only living thing who could possibly hear it is the horse at the bottom of our road. And to think we haven't even hit adolescence yet.

The awful thing is, I don't know that you ever entirely outgrow the capacity to be embarrassed by your parents, the ridiculous but visceral sensation that whatever they do or say in public will attract every eye in the place to yourself. Only the other day I was out with my mother at some function and she said she thought she would just point out to the organizers a small historical detail they had got wrong.

'Oh Mum,' I said. 'Mum, don't. Mum, please. Don't embarrass me.'

March, 1997

Speechless

My reflections on embarrassment a fortnight ago provoked what I suppose was a predictable plea from my eldest: 'Please, please don't write any more about me. It's embarrassing.' Not that he would dream of reading anything I write, but his pals do, and they can spot even the most veiled reference at a hundred paces, so he says. His life, in short, is not worth living.

My mother's comments on the same piece was that it was all very well going on about parents embarrassing their children, but what about daughters who without a by-your-leave go landing their mother in it every time she opens a newspaper? She's still smarting from the revelation of her immoderate excitement when her grandson mastered the word 'bum', and was noticeably restrained in my presence the other day when he came out with 'poo'.

Even my husband says he's fed up with strangers sidling up to him and saying archly, 'You don't know me, but I know all about you.' He got particularly broody a few months back when someone asked him out of the blue about our red Aga. Not one of the world's great pillow exclusives, I would have thought, but it bothered him. 'It's just disconcerting when someone you don't know from Adam knows the colour of your cooker,' he complained.

But you see, oh family of mine, this personal column lark is just not possible without victims. And when your home life is the whole point of it, for heaven's sake, what is a girl to do? Mind you, friends and acquaintances also get twitchy. 'You won't be putting this in the paper, will you, ha ha ha?' they say, the nervous laugh cutting right across the opening paragraph that was at that moment taking delicious shape in your head.

My head is full of paragraphs that never get written. I envy the sang-froid of Zoe Heller, the New York-based *Sunday Times* columnist who is wildly indiscreet, wickedly honest about the shortcomings of friends, neighbours, family, blameless strangers, indeed anyone at all who swims innocently into her ken – and completely safe in the knowledge that no one within several thousand miles will ever read it.

But this is Scotland, and it's small, and you can be sure that the woman at dinner whom you've just described as having 'this freaky Michael Jackson nose and a bizarre puff of platinum hair on top of her shrunken head' (one of my favourites from Heller) will be the first person you bump into in Boots next week or find yourself sitting next to in the London shuttle. This is a powerful brake on the runaway pen.

So it's back to the family, sitting targets one and all, along with anyone foolhardy enough to stumble into our orbit – like the lodger, for instance, an old friend who lives in mortal fear of straying into this column, but buys us such nice whisky and puts up so uncomplainingly with never knowing which passing traveller he'll find installed in his bed when he gets back after the weekend, that I can't bring myself to do it to him. Well, not this time, anyway.

There is, however, one person who never complains about getting a mention, for the simple reason that he's in no position to complain about anything. And that's just the problem. If only he would learn a few words, he could make his feelings about a lot of things clear, but my youngest is a child who simply will not talk.

This is a new one on me. I thought I'd been through most of the permutations in child development. I've had early walkers and late ones; I've supervised potty training that lasted anything from one day to several fraught months; I've had infants who'll eat everything and one who would eat nothing unless it had Farley's powdered chicken dinner sprinkled over it; I've got one son who regularly has to be ordered to leave some broccoli for the rest of us and another who manages to retch every time anything green so much as caresses his lips. But one thing they did all do: they were blethering happily well before the age of two.

These days I seem to find myself surrounded at every turn by toddlers of the same age as my silent son conversing with what I can only describe as brilliant fluency. Diminutive playmates whom he, marshalling the full resources of his vocabulary, labels patronizingly as 'baba', turn round and ask with impeccable syntax if he could see his way to getting out of that bubble-car and letting them in.

Apart from a couple of lavatorial expressions and today's new word, 'Goal!', all doubtless reflecting current priorities in our household, he's still working with the handful of words he first mastered over a year ago, when he was about nine months old and I was smugly assuming he would be reading *The Times* by the time he was two.

His siblings, who have been waiting with bated breath since he was about five weeks old to hear their names lisped prettily, are still waiting. Meanwhile he has coined some bizarre improvisations that make no attempt to imitate the real name but do seem to serve his purposes fine. One brother is Wawa and another is Dadda, which leads to considerable confusion with the other Dadda. His sister is Nana, an appellation she shares with one grandmother, a great-aunt, the au pair and any passing banana. The eldest brother is deeply hurt that he alone remains nameless and is still summoned by a meaningful stare or one of a vast array of grunts.

I suppose the floodgates will open soon and then I'll be lamenting the loss of my baby. And just as the exquisite sweetness of his first 'Mamma' began to lose its charm when it was being whinged at me day and night in an unstoppable litany, I dare say I'll be begging before long for relief. But I have to say it – right now a bit of variation from 'poo', 'bum', 'more' and tractor' would do me nicely.

Just as long as he doesn't start complaining about his mother's columns.

March, 1997

179

Spending a Franc

The Easter holidays seem a long time ago already: nothing to remind us of that epic drive to London except the forest of Hula Hoops underneath the car seats, the dog-eared Donkey cards and torn *Beano*s, the bubble-gum stuck under the dashboard, and the general air of a car that has seen action in worse places than Martin Bell could dream of.

This expedition was undertaken because I had committed myself to a morning's work in London but had no one to look after the gang at home. It seemed a good idea at the time to install myself at the wheel and take everyone with me, in a rather exotic twist to the BBC's Take Your Daughter to Work scheme. Take your daughter and her four brothers and drive 400 miles to get there. Well, why not?

Six truculent and increasingly desperate hours later, we arrived at my sister's house in Hammersmith. I had set out in early evening, with the youngest ones fully kitted out with pyjamas, blankets and pillows, in the fond expectation that they would all spend the journey in serene slumber. In fact, no one except the baby slept before Birmingham and then, just as the others were dropping off, we had to stop for petrol, which woke him up. He then screamed so loudly that he awakened everybody else again. I missed a vital interchange and ended up on the wrong motorway.

We stumbled in around 1 a.m. to find that my sister and her family had only just got back from a holiday in Costa Rica, where her husband was working. She was looking considerably perkier after a sixteen-hour flight with three children aged five, three and two than I was, but then she's that sort of girl. She once climbed Everest in her spare time, thinks nothing of whisking the offspring to the other side of the world at a moment's notice and, most impressive of all in my view, spends many happy weeks every summer in a mouse- and spider-infested French cottage with no washing machine.

She has always been like this. When we used to go on merry bachelor girl holidays together, she would stride off in the Mediterranean sun at noon to explore an interesting-looking hill, while I snoozed in a lounger. She married a television director specializing in anthropological films about people in jungles with no clothes on, and they are never happier than when doing intrepid things involving travel, heat and creepy-crawlies.

Her holiday anecdotes are always hair-raising, and this time was no exception. Comparing notes the next morning, my litany of seat-belt blues on the M6 paled pathetically beside her tales of a giant hermit crab biting one child's finger, another child's hand being vigorously clasped in the capacious beak of a toucan, and a ghastly night in their jungle cabin far from any hospital waiting to see if the three-year-old would wake up after a dramatic fall off a table in a Montezuma café. 'We lay there listening to the howler monkeys making their eerie wailing noise at dawn,' she told me with some relish, 'not knowing if he was in a coma, not able to get help if he was. And it seemed like it was the howl of death.'

It certainly beats running out of apple juice on the M1.

My other sister also outdid me on holiday anecdotes. She and my mother arrived back from France a few days ago still goggling at their experience with one of those automatic toilets on the platform at Cannes station. They're like big metal huts with green and red buttons on the outside, with a slot for your two-franc piece and copious instructions which my mother was attempting to decipher without her glasses while my sister paid her two francs and nipped inside.

Inside, reports my sister, it was like a Tardis with a damp floor, a hole in the ground and a metal bar you pulled down and sort of hovered over. She got out as fast as she could and, like any good Scot who would rather spend one penny than two, held the door open for my mother, who was still peering closely at the French print and had clearly not reached the bit which explained that between each use, the toilet will hose itself down.

In she went and the door closed with a thud. Immediately the red light began to flash menacingly. From inside came the sound of a roaring river in spate and terrified thumps on the metal walls, accompanied by muffled yells of 'Help! Help! Let me out.'

'I had no idea what was happening,' says my sister. 'I thought she was being drowned. I was shouting to her to keep calm, not to worry, and desperately stuffing two-franc pieces into the slot until suddenly the green light came on, the door burst open and she fell out. I was so relieved she wasn't dead that I started to laugh. Then I noticed that the entire station was laughing. People were hanging out of trains, guffawing across the platform. It's obviously a daily sport, watching foreigners cope with these toilets.'

On emerging from her ordeal, the bedraggled victim squelched over to a couple chortling quietly nearby and opened her heart to them with the immortal words: 'Oh, I wish I was back in Scotland.'

With such competition, there is not much worth reporting about my three-day trip to London. I got my work done, we spent time with friends and neighbours from our previous southern life (an experience which so confirmed my eldest in his Anglophile prejudices that he announced that even the sandwiches were better in England) and my husband at last showed up and took the children on what he billed as a sight-seeing trip round the historical sights of London: they spent the afternoon in Hamley's. This so exhausted him that when we drove back that night, he slept most of the way.

No one else did.

April, 1997

183

Kisses

I knew the beginning of the end had come when my first-born looked up from a *Smash Hits* edition on the Spice Girls, graciously accepted my proffered peck on the cheek and then asked thoughtfully: 'Why do people give each other good-night kisses?'

I was just launching into an ardent peroration on the subject when light dawned. 'Why?' I asked suspiciously. 'Don't you like them any more?'

'No,' he said mildly, burrowing back into the deathless prose.

I waited for him to look up again with a grin, throw his arms around my neck and murmur: 'Only joking, Mum.'

But he didn't. His final word as I reached the door was to ask what being arrested for disorderly behaviour meant.

I retreated into the next bedroom and buried the small, wry flicker of hurt in the neck of my drowsy five-year-old, who snuggled into the crook of my arm and sighed happily. How long before he, too, decides it's time for the kissing to stop?

Mind you, I am prepared to admit that I may overdo it a bit. As I went round the house last week pulling children from sofas, computers and trees to deliver a hefty smacker on each, one son observed with some exasperation: 'Why do you have to kiss every single one of us before you go, Mum? You're only off to Tesco's.'

But that's nothing. I can instigate a round of kisses before a trip to the bottom of the garden. Tips of noses, napes of necks, eyes, even the odd infant bottom if you're allowed to admit such a fetish these days – I need my fix. The two-year-old, with all those soft downy places that simply demand to be nuzzled, is particularly vulnerable to sudden maternal swoops, but nobody is safe. No wonder we're seeing the first signs of rebellion in the older ranks.

I've never been much of a one for social kissing. Lips skiting across a stranger's cheek leave me cold and I've never really got the hang of the flamboyant continental double-cheek stuff which doesn't seem to have caught on too much in Scotland but is big in metropolitan London. You never remember the second kiss is coming, which leaves the greeter pouting into mid-air and then lots of blushing apologies as you try and deliver the belated second one back on a cheek that has already moved. Give me a good old handshake any day.

I'm not even all that big on kissing children in general. Not even babies. Before the universe-cracking upheaval of giving birth to a child of my own, I would never have dreamed of so much as peeping into a pram and admiring the contents. Babies seemed to me, if I thought about them at all, rather ugly, noisy, ill-behaved creatures. When I decided to have one of my own, I worried that I might not love it.

But then, of course, I discovered – as most of us do – that I did love it; that I loved it more than anything on this earth, with a passion, a fierce unremitting intensity unlike anything I had ever felt before. I reclined in the hospital bed with this baby sprawled on top of me, his head bruised and squashed, his skin blotchy and one eye stuck shut, and thought he was the most beautiful being I had ever encountered. I looked pityingly at the other mothers who had been landed with such ugly babies and thought how they must envy me my paragon. I devoured him with kisses.

And each time it has been the same. Mother-love, they call it. Instant, overwhelming, ferocious, all-consuming. And blow me if I don't still want to keep devouring them with kisses. Is this a medical complaint and do I need help? Will I still feel this way when they're thirty, forty, fifty? Will I be chasing after them in the zimmer frame to demand one last hug before they leave the old dear?

Anyway, for the time being I'm still on safe ground with most of them. One son informed me the other day that he hated all kisses except mine. 'The stuff they do on the telly is yucky,' he said, emphatically. His younger brother also last week announced his firm intention of never getting married 'because I don't want to kiss anyone on the mouth ever'. Meanwhile their sister, who last night watched *The Sound of Music* on video for what she claims was the seventh time, insists on fast-forwarding it through the kissy bits. As Christopher Plummer moves in for the big one, she darts from her seat to the video button with an imprecation invariably drawn from their wide and varied vocabulary in this area: 'Yuk.'

Fortunately, at this end of the family maternal demonstrations of affection are still in favour, so I don't need to cut back all at once. I'll take it gently. As a first step I'll try a trip to the paper shop without a round of kisses, and maybe move on to letting them walk the dog without encountering a barricade of hugs at the front door. Then I may see if I can ease off the hail of kisses fired down the line every time I talk to one of them on the phone.

My husband is having to watch his own displays of affection on the telephone too these days. He got so into the habit of returning my effusively blown kisses that he recently found himself blowing a couple of resounding smackers down the line to his bank manager. He staggered into the kitchen wiping his brow and wondering if he should phone back to apologize. It was all my fault, he said.

No, there's nothing for it. I'm going to steel myself to hold back, cut down, ease off and in general stop being so pathetically soppy. I really am. But first, there's a squishy fat toddler around the house somewhere, with a little soft place under his chin that I just need to go and investigate. After all, a wee kiss never did anyone any harm, did it?

May, 1997

Double Lives

It was encouraging to see those pictures of Blair's Babes the other week, all bright-suited and eager and ready to go to war on the Westminster toilets.

It was equally satisfying to watch my erstwhile colleague Jeremy Paxman swinging into top hectoring gear and being treated to indulgent smiles instead of male bombast. The only way of torpedoing Paxman is not to take him seriously, and only women appear to understand this.

But the moment that crystallized for me what the brave new dawn for women at Westminster actually means was a single shot in the television news of Harriet Harman emerging from the Department of Social Security after her first day in office with a pile of folders up to her chin and the reporter's voice-over chirping about how she'd be up late tonight with all that homework. The next day it emerged that Harriet was to be Minister for Women as well, a little hobby to be pursued in her spare time between reforming the welfare system and getting a few hundred thousand people back to work.

I'll bet she trailed out to the official car that day with her feet killing her, wondering if she'd have to rustle up a pasta for the family supper, hoping that her children's homework wouldn't interfere too much with hers, mentally surveying who was going where that evening, who needed collecting, who would require clean sports gear the next morning, whether anyone had remembered to wash the last lot and which child was in the middle of this week's emotional crisis.

I've no idea what her domestic arrangements are, but I feel for her. She's got the power, the status, the red boxes and the satisfaction of making it to the top, but she must be knackered.

While her male colleagues can work as hard as they like, as long as they like, and then go off to relax with a glass of whisky or a seat at the Old Vic, quietly confident – in that maddeningly detached way that seems to come with the gender – that the children back home are safe, healthy, emotionally secure and in no danger of forgetting their lunch money, she can work only as hard as the minutiae of her three children's lives allow and only as far as her husband's New Mannish credentials extend, and she will doubtless find she can't even relax in the bath without someone banging on the door to ask her to come and find a lost roller-blade.

And then there's the change of pace. How do you cope with barking orders at civil servants all day and then getting home to find you need to ask the same question four or five times before anyone even registers that you've spoken?

I was thinking about this the other day when I arrived back from a live television broadcast, adrenaline still pumping from a job where everything is geared to concentrating hard, listening carefully and getting it right first time. How unlike the situation in my own dear home. Practically before my coat was off my back I found myself in the middle of the sort of scene that is played out a hundred times a day in different forms.

'Rice Krispies or Corn Flakes?' I asked. No reply. 'Which cereal would you like, I said, Rice Krispies or Corn Flakes? . . . Are you listening? Look at me to show you're listening. Which is it to be? . . . If you don't hurry up and tell me, you'll get nothing . . . No, we don't have Coco-Pops . . . Because I didn't buy any. Would you hurry up and answer me.'

This last comes out slowly, between gritted teeth through which a hint of the irritability which has already started to overwhelm the

190

pleasure of being back in the bosom of the family is starting to creep.

A short time later, with an older cast, we have the cheese sandwich syndrome. 'Look, it's great that you can go into the kitchen and make it yourself, saves me a lot of trouble, but please could you wrap up the cheese afterwards and put it back in the fridge? . . . No, if you put it there, you'll knock the yoghurt out . . . What did I tell you? And when you've picked up the yoghurt, do you see that little orange forest under the table, could you remove it? . . . No, don't just swipe it under the linoleum. Please go and get a brush . . . Did I not ask you five minutes ago to brush up that cheese? . . .'

And so on. Nothing unique in those scenes, but moving from an environment where you murmur, 'You couldn't be an angel and grab me a coffee, could you?' and find it magically by your hand the next time you look, to one where it takes fully ten minutes of arguing, entreating, demanding and finally ordering to get your eldest to clear his desk of gerbil sawdust before he starts his maths homework, is a bit of a culture shock.

Any working mother must find it so. Whatever the job, the pace of life at home takes some adjusting to. That doesn't necessarily mean going from fast to slow, high-powered to sluggish. Nothing in my working life, for instance, is as frenetic as an evening spent tearing around trying to satisfy the conflicting demands of my children's social diaries.

But it does mean being more prepared than I often am to go at their pace without fracturing my temper. The toddler needs his interminable ball game, the five-year-old needs a parent with the time and the divinely sent patience to read him *There's a Hippopotamus on Our Roof Eating Cake* every night for two weeks, the older ones have the right to expect you to be there and ready to listen for as long as it takes when the adolescent bluster suddenly evaporates and it's time to talk.

I bet Harriet Harman knows this as well as any of us. Which is why, for all my glee at the advance of the sisterhood into the corridors of power, I felt just a teensy bit sorry for her as she trailed to

191

the official car with her big pile of homework on that first heady
day in office.

May, 1997

Passion for Latin

The mother of one of my son's classmates phoned the other evening. She had heard on the grapevine that I shared her passion. Would I speak of it? Did I know of any others who were silently harbouring this love that dare no longer speak its name?

Yes, it's time to come out at last. I am one of those parents who want their children to learn Latin. I know of more, many more. And I will happily say it out loud, so that others will perhaps add their voices and the message will percolate through to the head teachers of the secondary schools who, one by one, are so casually robbing pupils and future pupils of a great treasure.

I wonder if those heads realize what a jewel they are casting aside when they cancel the Latin courses and boot the classics teachers into early retirement. Do they do it with heart-searching and regret, overwhelmed by the pressures of an overloaded curriculum and underloaded budget, or are they only too happy to junk a subject in which they never saw much point anyway? Either way, Latin is in its death-throes and many of us who believe in the importance of children being offered access to the civilization that formed our own and to the analytical language skills that facilitate the use of our own tongue and others, are watching in complicit silence.

So many of us regret the demise of Latin, but not so many have the time, the energy, the nous to organize the kind of parental campaign that might persuade the head teachers of big schools with big headaches to think again. So we try to persuade ourselves that it maybe doesn't matter much in this brave new semi-literate world, where we need all our energy to plant the occasional book under juvenile noses and guard the punctuation of the simplest English sentence. We forget that Latin is integral to that battle. And so it dies, murdered by ignorance and indifference.

Little did I think, when I sat all those years ago chanting *amo, amas, amat* and ready to climb the wall with the tedium of it all, that I would be arguing today for the opportunity for my children to climb it too. Yet even then, through the mist of conjugations and declensions and all the 'Lo, Tiberius is hastening to the market' stuff, I was beginning to get an inkling of why it mattered.

I remember the excitement of realizing how easily I could decode English words by stripping them to their Latin roots. I remember the sense of dawning mastery of language as I began to understand how words related to one another and what made a sentence elegant. The experience of learning Latin forced you to wrestle with the structures of language until you could see the logic. It required you to analyse; it required you to think. It was difficult.

But difficult studies are not in fashion these days. The vogue is not to get children to master structures and analyse patterns, so that they can build their own or a foreign language from understood foundations, but to encourage them to express themselves. This means, as far as I can gather, that as long as they can order a Coke in some fictional continental café, it doesn't matter too much whether they can construct a French or German sentence confidently and correctly from scratch. By the time it does matter, it's often too late to acquire the skills.

Similarly, the progressive undermining of English grammar means that children who can wax lyrical in a free-style poem may never understand the difference between a full-stop and a comma. The best teachers have always known that the most liberated and truly creative self-expression needs tools, and rules, which you can only throw away once you've learned how and why they work. But too many children are left with nothing but the haziest idea of how their language is structured.

For how can children possibly assimilate the rules of grammar without anyone teaching them? And how can they apply codes of language to a second language – in which they're 'immersed' for no more than a few hours a week – when they have no idea how their own works?

It's no wonder that you have students arriving at university unable to construct an essay, students aiming for an MA in German with only the vaguest notion of how to string a sentence together, and many youngsters leaving school without even the elementary command of language they need to be able to write a job application.

In the flight from boredom and difficulty, rote-learning and regurgitated facts, in pursuit of the exciting, the relevant, the idiomatic and the modern, we have recklessly thrown the baby out with the bathwater. Instead of merely refining the teaching techniques to engage and stimulate rather than bore rigid, we appear to be getting rid of the concept of mental discipline altogether. And off with it down the plug-hole is Latin, its decline symptomatic of the progressive devaluing of those things that cannot be immediately classified as relevant, utilitarian and fun.

Actually, even here they've got it wrong, because as the Government's own guidelines point out, Latin is of enormous practical use in the early years of secondary school, not just in helping with English and modern language work, but with scientific terminology and analytical thinking. And, as I'm told by those pupils who have been fortunate enough to get a taste of Latin from a good teacher before their school swept it away, these days it can actually be rather enjoyable.

What we're talking about here is not some deadbeat study of the past, but equipping our children for a new century in which no amount of computer literacy will eradicate the need for trained minds, linguistic skills and an understanding of the roots of their own culture.

The educational tide is turning in other areas, but probably not quickly enough for Latin. Once the last school has closed the last classics department, we will never get it back – and that can't be far off now, unless someone takes a stand. The Government would be doing Scottish education a great service if they at the very least insisted on one school in every area offering a shared opportunity to study Latin. There need to be some rules on Latin before it's too late.

July, 1997

Stimpy's Last Stand

I don't believe I ever mentioned the coming of Stimpy the gerbil to our household. Didn't have much of a chance, really, seeing as how his arrival was followed so very swiftly by his departure.

Even in a family not renowned for longevity among its pets, I have to admit two weeks was not a great innings. Only a couple of last year's goldfish, and the tadpoles who were unceremoniously transplanted a few days ago from the burn to a teetering bucket on our windowsill and who unaccountably failed to thrive on a diet of left-over chicken and boiled cabbage, have lasted a shorter time.

We all became rather fond of Stimpy in his brief sojourn among us. I was well disposed to him from the start, because I had struck a bargain with the eldest son requiring that he both kept his room tidy and fed the dog twice a day for two weeks before I would consider placing another animal in his exclusive care. And what a halcyon fortnight that proved to be. His room gleamed and so did the dog, who was clearly much gratified by this new regular feeding policy, removing from her as it did the responsibility of having to spend the evening looking soulful until somebody remembered.

As for the bedroom, well, it never occurred to me in those two weeks to wonder how a boy who had never in all his eleven years shown the remotest understanding that bookshelves might be intended for books, that a carpet of smelly socks and grubby shirts lacks something in the aesthetics department, or that drawers were on the whole designed for putting things in, was suddenly able to sustain for so long a pristine desk and a floor you could actually walk across.

It was only when he started to complain that he had no clothes left and I realized I hadn't washed anything of his for days that I looked more closely. Stashed under his bed I found books, papers, comics, useless felt-tip pens, pots of dried paint, coins, pencil shavings, Warhammer models, half-finished maths homework, and practically every piece of clothing he possessed in a state of advanced ripeness.

But by that time the deal had been completed. A diminutive white rodent had taken up residence in the second-hand cage in the corner of his bedroom, which was soon restored to its former glory as a midden, enhanced by the copious quantities of sawflakes that were soon spilling out of the cage and all over the carpet. This, I was informed, was entirely my fault for being too mean to buy a new cage with a proper plastic gerbil-house, which meant the animal was being forced to nest in a lowly corner where the bedding got pushed through the bars. Everyone who went into the room to visit the gerbil trailed some out with them, until the house became a sea of wood shavings. This is something the friends who advised me that gerbils were 'no trouble' did not see fit to mention.

Yet even being forced to trail the vacuum cleaner up the stairs more times in a day than I usually care to in a week did not dent my affection for young Stimpy. As mice go – and let's not get hung up on species here; I know a mouse when I see one – he was a pleasant wee soul who, against all the odds, appeared to enjoy the rough and tumble of life in our family circus. He certainly did nothing to deserve getting eaten.

It happened at teatime. There was a terrible scream from upstairs and a moment later the eldest crashed into the kitchen, launching into a lifetime's best performance for which many years of amateur melodramatics had prepared him so well. This time, though, I had to hand it to him: the occasion lived up to the delivery. His room, he roared, had been ransacked. Someone had broken into the cage. The gerbil had gone. We had to find Stimpy.

We all rose like a great avenging wave from the table, thundered upstairs and stopped, awestruck, on the threshold of his room. The detritus of battle was everywhere: sawflakes scattered by the ton, the contents of the litter bin sprayed over the carpet, the duvet dragged off the bed, the cage battered and empty. We stood aghast, the same thought in every mind. Dog.

'We have to find Stimpy,' his owner pleaded again. But the words died on his lips as each one of us, by some grim instinct, suddenly found our eyes focusing on something in the middle of the devastated carpet. A pathetic little heap of red innards. No skin, no head, no tail. 'She'll be sick tonight and I'll have to clean that up too,' I found myself thinking bitterly.

Oh ungrateful hound, was two weeks of regular feeding not enough for you? Did you have to make your point quite so, well, *carnally*?

We all just stood there, absorbing the realization that this wee mess of guts was all that was left of the bright-eyed creature whom half an hour ago I had requested be removed from the kitchen table or they'd get droppings for tea.

The two eldest flung themselves into my arms in a storm of grief. The daughter, who last year went in for the full histrionic works when her goldfish died, proved rather more flinty on this occasion and raced off to announce the news to a younger brother who had missed the drama. With no concessions to euphemism and more than a hint of relish, she reported that Bonnie had eaten the gerbil.

So, another funeral, another grave, another cross beneath the tree . . . and fresh thoughts on the fate of our long-lamented rabbit, whom we liked to imagine having run off last year to populate the hillside with nice little bunnies. Now we're not so sure.

But it certainly reminded us to give the dog her dinner that night. Not that she needed it.

July, 1997

199

Heavy Labour

I have just been back to the Queen Mother's. Kind friends with my welfare and sanity at heart will be reassured to know that this visit to Scotland's largest maternity hospital was for purely professional purposes. But I have to admit there was one moment of the gravest danger.

This was not at the sight of all those small, clean, sweet-smelling bundles of baby, whom I managed to pass with barely a flicker of desire. No, it was the delivery room that did for me. It was not one of the deluxe suites in the new wing with a corner bath, television and enough easy chairs to put the family up for a fortnight. This one was cramped and unprepossessing, full of tubes and bits of alarming-looking equipment, with a second door opening through to a rear corridor that the staff are pleased to refer to as the back passage.

Hardly the sort of place, you'd have thought, to make the pulses race and the hormones whirl and a veteran mother's thoughts turn lightly to having another one. I mean, the magnificent staff at the Queen Mum's did their best, but we're talking pain here, lots of it, the wall-climbing, partner-battering, please-just-let-me-die sort that you'd think might rather put you off repeating the pleasure.

But this is the extraordinary trick that Nature plays on poor, defenceless women in its bid to perpetuate the species. Before anyone's even had time to hose down the walls and help your husband rub the blood off his natty white trainers, amnesia has started to set in. As the months pass, you remember it was painful but catch yourself thinking of it as a rather bracing experience.

'Bracing?' said my husband with a hollow laugh. 'That's not the way I remember you expressing it at the time.' It's not the way I remember expressing it at the time either. This ridiculous dilution of memory must be why the comforting birth gurus of the National Childbirth Trust, who have had babies of their own and should surely know better, are able in all conscience to advise innocent souls at their antenatal classes that a useful tip for making it through labour without any nasty drugs or epidurals is to lie back and think of a flower opening.

I can't vouch for the rest of my classmates of the NCT group in Maidenhead, 1985, but that's certainly not what I was thinking of when I lay back with my legs in stirrups, a couple of strapping midwives holding on for dear life at the top end and a dishy registrar at the other hauling at my insides with a pair of giant salad servers while remarking pleasantly that he recognized me from television. (Which bit of me exactly? The great thing about being so comprehensively away with the fairies in labour is that the toe-curling embarrassment doesn't hit you till later.)

That birth was not at the Queen Mother's. Only the fifth was born there, by which time I should have been popping them like peas. But you show me a pea of 9lb 12oz. I moaned and yelled and gulped down the gas-and-air and giggled drunkenly and wanted to die. Yet the other day I gazed upon the scene of my torture and wondered if I had been making a bit of a fuss about nothing. I thought how wonderful it had felt when the hammer-blows stopped, remembered the euphoria when I cradled that new, soft, unutterably beautiful baby for the first time. 'You're off your head,' said my husband.

I had better be careful what I write here. A correspondent told me she once sent a column of mine to her sister in England, who was so affected by something I had written about babies with downy heads snuggling into your neck that she promptly went off and conceived her fourth.

This is a big responsibility, so in case I have inadvertently set any maternal hormones racing this time, let me remind you of what I was only too soon able to remind myself: what you're in for when the euphoria dissipates and the baby reveals itself not only to have the right number of fingers and a cute nose, but an equally perfectly functioning digestive system, is a life – if you'll forgive me – of shit.

I speak from the heart. In over eleven years of child-rearing, I have only enjoyed about fifteen months without nappies, a period amply compensated for by all the months when I had two lots on the go. At some £6 a week, I reckon I must have swelled the Pampers company coffers by around £3,500.

The feelings of gentle broodiness I had been nursing happily on the way back from the Queen Mum's lasted just about the hour it took to collect the two-year-old from home and pop along to a friend's house for a cup of tea. This child and I are currently involved in that ancient ritual known as potty training. It's a process with many phases, of which no one who has done it will wish to be reminded, but at some point it involves taking your courage in your hands – and a lot more, if you're not careful – and venturing out in public with only a wispy pair of underpants between you and a very big mess.

I think I managed two gulps of tea before the first alarm, which finished off the underpants. The second call led to feverish scrubbing of the nice beige bathroom carpet, whereupon my friend tactfully suggested we might all adjourn outside so that the youngster could do his worst *au naturel*. With free run of the extremely ample garden, he chose a spot right next to the table laden with mugs of replenished tea and chocolate cake to deposit his next small and perfectly formed pile.

There are moments when you go off even the most delicious home baking. These are also the moments when mothers of five who should have known better stop being even the teeniest, weeniest bit broody.

Thank heaven for little swirls.

July, 1997

Arran

Well, we did it at last. After eleven years of avoiding these places at all costs, we finally dared the unthinkable. We took the troops to a hotel.

Actually it was a guest house, which is even more brave now that I think about it, because there is nowhere to hide, no wall that an infant tantrum will not pierce, no corner of the dining room where an innocent guest will not be blasted by the latest squabble.

But we did it. I may be basking in blissful ignorance of the things our fellow guests were really saying about us, but I must say it did seem to go rather well. The combination of novelty, dire threats and the most child-friendly hosts you could hope for produced such tolerably civilized meal-times that there was even the odd moment when I was conscious of a strange sensation.

As the five-year-old made himself at home by talking animatedly to his cutlery, the two-year-old quietly got on with transferring the entire contents of the butter dish to his plate and mixing it with the mountain of pepper he had already deposited there, and the older three tucked into their meal with genuine relish, murmuring (with a smug glance in my direction) a polite thank-you or two as they passed the potatoes, I realized what the feeling was. Relaxation.

It was only fleeting, mind you. The youngest was soon empire-building and started to manoeuvre his pepper mountain on to my tenderly poached salmon. His brother said goodbye to his fork and announced loudly that there was something funny about these potatoes. Further up the table a discussion about how we were going to spend the evening started to get heated. Still, we survived the experience with stress levels not much higher than normal, and so – I hope – did the rest of the dining room.

I've decided that the secret of this rather delightful holiday was simple. We kept it short. Very short. Two days, actually.

You may laugh, but look at it this way. More than two days and things are getting a bit obstreperous, especially if the weather is bad. Even a modest guest house will become expensive, too, when you multiply everything by seven. On the other hand, just a couple of days without buying, storing, cooking and clearing away food on the scale our family consumes it, with beds made and rooms tidied and fresh towels into the bargain, is worth a fortnight to me in any self-catering establishment you care to offer.

In fact, although we hit on two nights and three days simply because that was the only time my husband had off work and the nine-year-old was deeply worried about having nothing to write about in the post-holiday school essay if we didn't go somewhere, anywhere, for a while, our experience on the west coast isle of Arran has revolutionized my thinking about holidays. The children will be appalled to learn that I now consider two days to be the optimum length for a family holiday and will be advocating it vigorously in the future.

Of course, it all rather depends where you go. We fetched up by sheer accident with Pete and Barbara Rawlin at Viewbank House in Whiting Bay, and I defy anybody in the whole of Scotland to have landed luckier. They're the sort of hosts who smile brightly when you troop into their dining room straight from the beach, depositing half the sands of Kildonan on their carpet; who serve up exquisitely cooked fresh food for the adults but are not too proud to rustle up a quick sausage for the children; who offer to dry your sea-sodden T-shirts in their kitchen overnight and don't bat an eyelid when presented with a dripping pile as high as Goat Fell; who allow you to hang your manky beach-towels on their washing line and don't complain when the flapping keeps setting off the night-time intruder lights.

It also helps when you strike lucky with the weather, although the beauty of these quick, spur-of-the-moment breaks is that you can actually consult a forecast before you decide to go for it. Who needs the stresses of charter flights and a stifling fortnight avoiding skin cancer on the Costa del Anywhere, when you can have two long, sparkling days on Arran?

When the sun is out, what more can you possibly want than that warm rock and glistening sea? Can the most sophisticated Mediterranean holiday clubs really beat an inflatable plastic dinghy in a sandy bay and a handful of cheap fishing nets? Can all the sights of Tuscany equal the magic of a school of dolphins dipping in and out of the gleaming water, so close that the most notoriously timid of our children decided they were after him and paddled furiously for the shore? Would all the joys of Disney really thrill as much as our hunt for the basking sharks and the momentous discovery of that first beady-eyed seal a few feet away?

Of course, all these delights pall in time, and indeed by the third day the skies were louring, one child was starting to mutter that he was fed up with beaches, and everyone pooh-poohed my suggestion of a brisk walk along the shore to pay homage at the Viking fort in favour of a happy hour choosing cap-guns and stink-bombs in the local shop.

But that's the beauty of the quick stay. By the time they and the weather are getting restive, the ferry is beckoning again, and we're all home before anyone has said the word 'bored' once.

What's more, it's maybe the only way of keeping your own childhood memories bright without deep disillusionment setting in. In Whiting Bay the gulls were still wheeling the way they did thirty years ago, the café on the hill was still serving Cokes from tables where you could watch the shifting shades of sea and sky, the Scripture Union was still belting out its brave beach hallelujahs and yes, crucially, the sun was still shining.

And we got out before it was too late.

August, 1997

Memory Loss

So it's back to school this week. Where on earth have the last six weeks gone? Already the whole period is a blur, which is a nuisance because I sat down here thinking I might squander a word or two on tales from the holidays, and now find that beyond our trip to Arran and a couple of magical afternoons at Loch Lomond, I can't actually remember doing anything at all.

This is doubtless another sign of the senility that has been encroaching apace ever since I started on the child-rearing business. Only yesterday I was trying on a pair of dolphin-shaped earrings presented by the second son. 'How do you like my sunglasses?' I asked the gang. 'What?' they all chorused. 'How,' I said, enunciating very slowly and carefully as one does for the slow-witted, 'do you like my new sunglasses . . . er, I mean earrings?'

The previous evening I ordered one of the children to hurry up and brush his teeth. Or I thought I did. What I actually said was 'Hurry up and get your seat-belt on', which he said was almost as funny as the time I was saying his prayers and asked God to bless my little orange juice. Neither of us can remember what I could possibly have meant to say that time, but if there's a consultant in geriatric medicine reading this, please don't be tempted to get in touch. I'd rather not know.

In fact, the greater part of the school holidays passed in much the same way as this morning. Daughter and her best friend are outside making what they describe as a sweetie machine; her two elder brothers are circling like vultures. Sure enough, as I write, the daughter is hurling herself across the garden, tears streaming down her face, with a piece of paper in her hand. The boys have slunk out of sight. She beats at the window and tosses in the paper, which reads: 'IF YOU EVER WANT TO SEE YOUR SWEETS AGAIN PAY 20P. LEAVE THE MONEY AT THE OUTSIDE TAP. IF YOU TELL, WE WILL EAT THEM! From Mr X and Mr Y.'

I'm now guarding on my desk here two lollipops, a Refresher, a chocolate football and a vile-looking pink Barbie bar. I'm also in possession of the ransom note, which has taken over the place on the desk only just vacated by the second-youngest's will, which I discovered him writing a few minutes ago.

This gave me quite a turn, since only last night he had been telling me tearfully before he went to bed that he'd rather not have any more birthdays because he never wanted to grow up to be a man. Why not? 'Because I don't want to have to kiss on the lips,' he wailed. 'I just want to go to heaven instead.'

When I asked him what he was writing so earnestly this morning, he answered airily, 'It's my will, of course.' There was a whole page of closely written mumbo-jumbo. 'What does it say?' I asked, reflecting that nowhere in Penelope Leach could I recall any advice for dealing with a suicidal five-year-old. 'I'll tell you when it's finished,' he said mysteriously. Then he added, to my considerable relief, 'It's for my treasure box. All pirates' treasure boxes have wills, you know.' Of course they do.

It's all very well enjoying these moments, but what's the point if I don't remember them in the future? Unless I write them down at the time, they're gone, like so much of the rest of my life of which I have an alarmingly hazy recall. I suppose I should keep a diary, but the nearest I've managed over the last few years is a notebook for jotting down memorable sayings . . . when I remember.

I see the last one was a thoughtful question from the five-year-old when I went in to kiss him good night one evening last April. He was silent so long I thought he was asleep, until suddenly a small voice penetrated the hush: 'Do octopuses fart?'

I did keep a real diary once, one of those five-year volumes which I started when I was thirteen and rediscovered the other day. I'm hoping to lose it again very soon. Reading it over my shoulder last night, the eldest son pronounced it 'sad'. 'No wonder you can't remember anything about your life, Mum,' he mused. 'It was much too boring to remember.'

He had a point. The early entries are a litany of minuscule ailments ('Today a definite improvement. I still felt sick but managed to eat a bit'), endless comments about the weather, complaints about homework and the tedium of double maths, and pathetic little triumphs like 'Scored a goal at hockey today. Super game.'

'Soooper game,' mimicked my son. 'Spiffing goal, what? For goodness' sake, Mum, you didn't really talk like that, did you?'

I didn't think I did, but I'm so appalled at the ghastly, moaning creature revealed in this monument to narcissism that I'm not sure what to believe.

And it gets worse. Adolescence in full spate, the diary full of weary worryings about the intractable problem of Boys. 'After last night's passionate embraces, I've gone right off Rolf. He just doesn't appeal the way he did; now I see him as wee and fat. Talked to him a bit, but managed to avoid him at the disco. How I hate kissing.'

I seem to recall getting over that little phobia all right, but I'd better warn the five-year-old it could take some time. In the meantime, amnesia is bliss and I'll stick with the present, in which eldest son and his pal from down the road are just passing the window clad in black balaclavas, with loaded water-rifles slung over their shoulders, heading with deadly intent for the sweetie machine. I'm counting down to the screams.

There is, however, one thing I do wish I could remember. Who the hell was Rolf?

August, 1997

211

Another Fine Mess

The other day I taught the five-year-old to ride a bike. I'm an old hand at this lark and the procedure is well established. First, mosey over to grandparents' house, where smooth driveway offers perfect conditions for the job.

Then push him around for a while till he gets the hang of it. Proceed to stand by with a box of Elastoplast saying portentous things like 'Everything that's worthwhile in life takes practice', or more often 'For goodness' sake, get up. Your sister never made a noise like that when she was learning.' Then at some point in the proceedings you feel confident enough in the skills you've so patiently imparted to slope off inside for a cup of tea, while the learner whizzes smugly round the garden.

It's a well-rehearsed routine, as I say, which has worked fine in the past. This time, though, there was one small difference. Careless of the hazards to which every stationary object in the garden was about to be exposed, I had parked the car at the front of the house.

When I returned from the tea-break to monitor progress, I discovered that my novice cyclist had found a new place to practise. 'Round the car is much more difficult, Mum,' he yelled over his shoulder as he teetered along the narrow path between the family wagon and the front window, executing before my very eyes a large and perfectly formed streak across the door with a handle-bar from which years of abuse by his siblings had long ago removed the rubber grip. I can still hear that scrape.

I looked again. Three gashes along the side. From the considerable body of experience I've acquired in this area over the years, I could see at once that this was a two-panel job.

Remarkably undaunted by being thundered at to get off that bike immediately and look at what he had done, the son remarked chirpily, 'Don't worry. The other side's easier. I'll just go round there instead.'

You have never seen a boy removed from his bike more quickly. I dragged him to the other side and stared, aghast, at a door that looked like one of the two-year-old's better drawings. Wobbly lines and delicate curves, a couple of perfect ticks, one gouged dot, all gleaming grotesquely in the sunshine. Maybe I could enter it for the Turner prize. 'You say this side was easier?' I screeched.

It's just as well that years of having practically everything we possess scraped, scratched, ripped, scribbled over, stampeded across, smashed, bashed, squashed or smeared with banana tend to deflate the materialistic instincts rather. I know people who might have suffered a stroke at the sight of that car, but me, I went back in and had another cup of tea.

There is, of course, the little matter of what it will cost to respray, or how much it will reduce the value of the car when we sell it, as my father-in-law keeps reminding me in the same exasperated tone that he reserves for pointing out that 'cars do need oil, you know', but as I see it, there's no point in thinking about that just yet because there are bound to be a few more dents before long anyway.

'Has your husband seen it yet?' people ask, with the quaint assumption that the man of the house is bound to view things like cars with their proper seriousness. But I feel on firmish ground here. He will, of course, come over all self-righteous and demand to know what I was thinking about parking there of all places, but in general he takes a rather relaxed view of child-induced trauma to the material things of life.

As he said the day the dog took a bite out of a newly upholstered family heirloom: 'Look at it this way. This sofa is full of memories. We're adding some more.'

Every fork-mark gouged in the kitchen table, every chair-spring that buckles under an enthusiastic bounce, every covert signature on the best wallpaper, every roller-blade scrape on the hall floor are, according to this way of thinking, memories to enjoy later. Sure, you bawl the children out for it and try to teach them to respect the things around them, but it makes for a more relaxing life not to mind too much when it happens. So we may well spend old age with our bottoms scraping the floor in springless armchairs, but we'll enjoy the memories.

This is not a philosophy that comes easy when you're rubbing a mashed custard cream out of your best jacket. Or contemplating the interesting patterns made by dripped blood down a heavy gold curtain that's just back from the dry cleaner's. Or leading a guest into what we optimistically call 'the best room' to find every piece of furniture pushed against the wall, the table upside down, the floor covered with popcorn and a circus in progress.

Still, better to laugh if you can. And we nearly always do in the end, as long as the children understand that one thing beyond all others is sacrosanct. Scrape my car, ruin my clothes, crash my computer, scratch my records and you'll live to maraud another day. But mess with my books and you've had it.

Even here, though, memory will probably triumph in the end. I received my first and virtually, I think, last smack from my own father at the age of two or three when I scribbled on an Icelandic book of his. We both remember it rather fondly these days, and the passion for books he was unleashing in that reprimand proved infectious.

In the end, perhaps a poet friend of mine called Steve Turner put it best when he wrote once:

These are
the good
old days.
Just wait
and see.

September, 1997

This Is Your Life

It's been a hectic time. First there was *This Is Your Life*, which my mother had consented in a weak moment to land my father in and which involved a family exodus to London to give him the sort of surprise he could probably have well done without.

The television company put us up in a hotel in Regent's Park seething with media types, including the entire ABC News operation, who were preparing for the funeral of Diana, Princess of Wales, the following Saturday. To reach the rooms we had to pick our way along corridors crammed with camera boxes, cables and production assistants sitting cross-legged on the carpet typing scripts about grief.

The rooms had doors which shut so fast that we all kept locking ourselves out. Once I managed to do it with both the key and the two-year-old inside, and had to race back along the news corridor, down in the lift and wait in an interminable queue at reception for a new key, frantically imagining the room on fire from electrical grief overload, or the child deciding to take a closer look at the open third-floor window.

The lifts were just as bad. They snapped shut as fast as the two-year-old's teeth on a biscuit. On our way out, three of the children stepped in and were suddenly whisked off into the stratosphere, while the rest of us set off on a Marx Brothers chase to find them. Correctly assuming that, although the eldest was one of the missing party, he would no more remember what floor he had started out from than he is likely to know what day it is or where he last left his shoes, I hurtled downstairs and placed the second eldest on guard on the ground floor. Carrying the youngest and dragging behind us the Czech au pair, whose English was never quite up to understanding what we were all doing in London anyway and whose air of startled distraction was growing by the minute, I zoomed up and down in another lift until we located the lost ones at last and hauled them down to the waiting taxi.

When we reached the television studios, the children were mercifully removed to a room with a video and a pile of sweets, while I set off to change into the glad rags I had shoved into a polythene bag before leaving, the challenge of dressing five children in those cramped Alcatraz bedrooms having been quite enough without having to do it for myself too. This arrangement would have worked well enough if I had remembered to include my shoes in the bag. Since the clumpy boots I had on were not the sort of thing in which one really wanted to glide down the catwalk to surprise the pater, I had to go padding around the assembling audience in bare feet trying to locate a friend with size five shoes who wouldn't mind handing them over sharpish. I eventually located an elegant black pair which were considerably nicer than the ones I had left at the hotel, and their owner settled down to watch the show in her stocking soles.

My siblings and I stood behind the big *This Is Your Life* doors waiting to be introduced, feeling incredibly foolish and quite unable to think of any conceivable reason why we had agreed to do this. We were all somewhat amazed to find that in the end we rather enjoyed the experience, mainly because we sensed that 'the subject', as they call the victim in these circles, was rising to the occasion and enjoying himself too. And there was a good party afterwards.

It's a twee programme, *This Is Your Life*, but I realize now that what it can do at its best is offer an opportunity for the sort of warm tribute you normally only get in an obituary, which by then is a bit over the subject's head, as it were. In a media world where it's always smarter to sneer, it is rather refreshing to hear genuine and unabashed expressions of respect and honour.

We all stayed on in London so that I could do my stint reporting for the BBC on the morning of Princess Diana's funeral. Walking through Kensington Gardens at 3.30 a.m., amid the vast sea of flowers lit by hundreds of flickering candles around the trees, was an unforgettable experience. Even at that hour dozens of people were wandering around, looking, talking quietly, or sitting hugging their knees in the candlelight in front of the photographs of Diana pinned to the trees.

'What's all the fuss about?' I heard one brave soul ask of the devotees at one such shrine. A girl with frizzy black hair turned to him from her seat on the grass: 'She was a being . . . a being. That's the only way to describe her.'

'But she was just like any of us. She had her faults,' ventured the brave one.

'What faults?' demanded a voice from the other side of the tree. It was a young man in a leather jacket. 'She didn't have any faults. It was that other lot that had the faults.'

The interlocutor gave up and lapsed into silence, shaking his head. Standing or sitting around the tree in front of the massed flowers, the pictures and the candles, the scrawled messages of adoration and pain, strangers were sharing their thoughts without reserve or embarrassment.

Whatever we decide in the end that the phenomenon of the reaction to Diana's death has meant, two aspects struck me forcibly in that pre-dawn walk in the gardens. First, the need to worship: the wholly genuine and unhysterical, but profoundly disturbing need to turn a nice woman with a beautiful face into a religious being. And secondly, the desire among people of all ages and backgrounds simply to come together to express what was in their hearts: a hunger for camaraderie. I'm not sure we can define any of that as grief, but as Tony Blair recognized very early on, it was powerful stuff.

A pity, I thought, that Diana would never know what they

thought of her. A pity, perhaps, that she never made it to *This Is Your Life* to hear the Queen saying she was remarkable.

September, 1997

220

Blinky Spots

'Have you ever considered plastic surgery?' the eldest son enquired lightly the other day. He had been watching a programme about it and reckoned it could do wonders for my chin.

'What's wrong with my chin?'

'Well, it sort of doubles up when you look down. You could get a little tuck in just at the back here, and your worries would be over.'

What worries? I didn't have any worries. Now I can hardly pass a mirror without forcing my chin into grotesque contortions to inspect what happens when I look down.

The daughter turned nervously to her brother. 'Do you think I need surgery too?' she asked, patting her own chin thoughtfully.

'Naw,' retorted the expert. 'It's only for the elderly.'

And that's another thing. In what is supposed to be the prime of life, I find myself being hustled unceremoniously into antiquity.

The six-year-old was at it last night as well. I had read him his favourite animal book and we were lying on his bed discussing the feeding habits of the babirusa and whether some strange Madagascan creature called the aye-aye might be called the aye-aye because its eyes are funny. On the whole, I was explaining, I thought not, when suddenly he fixed me with a long stare and said, 'You're looking a bit old. Your face is sort of red. And your spot is all' – he searched for the right word – 'blinky.'

Blinky? 'Yes, blinky. That's how spots go when you get old. Do aye-ayes blink?'

As if it wasn't bad enough having a double chin, a red face and a blinky spot, any pretensions to some lingering allure in my declining years were firmly quashed at breakfast this morning when I was rash enough to mention that I had found Tommy Lee Jones rather fanciable in the film *Men in Black*.

'But he's ancient,' said the eldest, in tones of genuine horror.

'Yes, but think of that craggy jaw, those pained eyes, that black suit,' I protested, having always been rather susceptible to the Mills & Boon type and determined to fight my corner. 'Older people can be very sexy, you know.'

'Well, *you're* not,' shot back the second eldest, adding, in a kindly attempt to soften the blow, 'Although maybe you used to be when you were young.'

I remember now how my mother used to complain that she only began to feel anything other than seventeen when we, her children, started treating her like a mental defective. Inside, she explained, she was still the girl who had leaped over a dustbin in Glasgow's Buchanan Street on her way to her first job interview with the editor of the *Sunday Post* in 1943. To herself she has always remained that girl who could take a dustbin in her stride; indeed, I think it was a bit of a shock to her not to have won the grandmothers' race at the primary sports last year.

It is always others who press our antiquity and our mortality upon us, and none more so than the next generation. I can remember as a child tagging along behind my mother in Rutherglen Main Street as she made a beeline for some wrinkled crone with the words, 'I must go and say hello to that girl.'

'How can you call that woman a girl?' I would demand.

'She's a girl to me,' was the invariable reply. 'She was in my class at school.'

Mind you, unlike my own children, I don't think I was ever aware as a child of my own mother ageing physically. Those grey-haired forty-somethings whom she embraced as contemporaries seemed a race and an age apart from my mother, who was simply herself, special, unique, in a sense ageless. It would never have occurred to me to notice whether her hair was changing colour or her face acquiring lines.

But today's children are so immersed in television adverts for smooth skin and glossy hair, in programmes about everything from plastic surgery to getting rid of spots, in the cult of perfect bodies and infallible youthfulness blasted at them wherever they go, that I suppose it's no wonder they turn their critical attention to the face that's nearest them most often.

And so we have the irony that, at a time when women – not averse to seduction by the odd advert themselves and able to see no earthly reason why they should go all matronly before they feel it – are looking younger, dressing younger and acting younger than ever before, they are probably more subject than ever before to being reminded in no uncertain terms that they are not. Young, that is.

All this proved so deeply depressing that I took myself off to the new Waterstone's bookshop in Glasgow. Bookshops always cheer me up, especially when the coffee is good, but here I made one fatal mistake. I bought a book about the Hay diet, which promises all sorts of wonderful things like endless energy and no double chins if you will only desist from eating your meat and your potatoes at the same meal.

Unfortunately the author finds it necessary to itemize everything your current diet is bound to have done to you, and a quick survey revealed that I am likely to be suffering from low blood sugar, food intolerance, candida and so many other things that it's clear there is much more to worry about than a blinky spot.

Old, spotty and disease-ridden. What chance now of prancing off into the sunset with Tommy Lee Jones?

September, 1997

Kitchen Capers

We're having the kitchen done. Yes, I know. Folly. 'Don't do it,' friends warned. 'It goes on for ever. You'll be a wreck before it's half finished.'

'Never fear,' I informed all and sundry, with that breezy confidence that is the hallmark of the truly naive. 'I have been assured that it will take four days maximum, with maybe an extra day or two for the floor and the paintwork. Tea at Burger King a few times and we'll be out the other side, no bother.'

You see before you a chastened woman. The Cassandras have of course been proved comprehensively right. Almost a month into the project I can feel a nervous tic developing behind the eye and a knot of tension building in the solar plexus, sensations hitherto unknown in the domestic arena, where I normally find benign neglect does wonders for peace of mind.

By yesterday evening it was seriously getting to me: the disruption, the mess, the dust, the ladders, the treks up and down to the back bedroom, where any visitor reckless enough to pass our way finds himself sleeping among food-mixers, pans, coffee sets, wine bottles, a giant wok and every crystal wedding present we've never dared use – in fact, everything we couldn't cram into the cubbyhole beside the washing machine from which we are currently conducting all culinary operations.

With the entire kitchen shrouded in drapes, I tried to rustle up the simplest thing I could think of for tea. It's only when you have to burrow under heavy dust-sheets to look for them that you realize just how many different items you need from different places to make a round of beans on toast. Knives and forks from drawer, beans from cupboard, loaf from dust-thick bread bin, toaster extricated from another corner, butter squeezed out from the back of the fridge, plates from shelf, every manoeuvre occasioning a great shroud-lifting pantomime which climaxed in a manic hunt for the tin-opener that finally brought the whole lot down on my head and the painter hurtling down his ladder to the rescue.

By the time I got this magnificent feast to the table, tripping over planks of wood left by the joiner and bending double under ladders, it was almost dark and, there being no lights installed yet and no socket near the table for a lamp, it was a gloomy business in more ways than one.

If the head of the family had been around, he would doubtless have lit a galaxy of candles and transformed it into a fun occasion. 'Let's have a party,' he'd have declared to the circle of children peering bleakly through the murk at yet another plateful of cheap Asda baked beans and muttering about some people being so mean they couldn't even buy Heinz. 'And a prize,' he'd have added, 'for the first person to make your mother see the funny side of this.'

But the said patriarch has hightailed it off on a working trip to Fiji where, he complained on the phone the other night, it has been raining since he got there and looks like Doncaster. My heart bleeds.

My own stock of the festive spirit is running just a touch low right now. I'm so fed up with the whole kitchen business that when my mother came on the phone after tea to say she had just watched a programme about the dangers of lead in old paint and wondered if there might be any in our venerable kitchen, I heard myself declaring hysterically: 'Look, I don't care if all the children get lead poisoning. I've got enough to think about.'

Of course, by the calmer light of day I do care, but since it's all been painted over now and any particles of lead are presumably either there being breathed in, or not there, and we'll never know which unless one of the children starts finding it difficult to learn his tables, I'm hanged if I can see what I can possibly do about it, except add it to the mental list of Things Mothers Worry About, along with electric pylons, food additives, BSE and the chances of the eleven-year-old reading a book between now and the year 2000.

A minute ago, as I drifted through the kitchen, the joiner informed me *en passant* that the boards we're putting on some of the walls have been banned in America. 'Why?' I enquired icily. 'Oh, when you cut them, they give off something that gives you cancer,' he said cheerfully. The plumber looked up from the radiator. 'Yup, I heard that too. Cancer. Mind you, it's just small amounts, I heard.'

Nothing like a nice new kitchen to cheer you up, I always say. Meanwhile my more pressing priority has been how to feed my parents-in-law, who put off their planned visit earlier in the month because of the upheaval and arrived a week after I had assured them it would be finished, armed with the not unreasonable expectation that they might be able to eat from time to time.

My father-in-law belongs to the three-cooked-meals-a-day school. He's a bacon and eggs, meat and two veg with Yorkshire pudding sort of chap, and beans on toast doesn't do a lot for him. He has borne his fate with fortitude, but I did detect a note of more than usually fervent sincerity when he remarked this morning that he looked forward to seeing the new kitchen on their next visit. I didn't like to tell him that, the way things are going, the Christmas turkey may well hang in the balance.

Still, at least we're out of it for a while now. We're off to Florida, leaving house, dog and fish, along with the unexpected bonus of joiner, painter, plumber and electrician, in the hands of a family who think they're coming to spend a quiet week in the country. It may be the end of a beautiful friendship.

October, 1997

Grave Difficulties

All right, so spending the afternoon in a cemetery where no one you know is buried would not head many lists of favourite Sunday afternoon activities.

And I grant you it was a considerable feat of persuasion to entice the entire family to do it, since 'walking', 'gravestones' and 'long-dead relatives of your Auntie Helen' are concepts difficult to sell to an eleven-year-old who is enjoying himself in front of a computer screen sowing death and destruction of a much more satisfying kind.

But he came. The nine-year-old was winkled out of the garden, the six-year-old prevailed upon to abandon his drawing, the two-year-old spun some yarn about treasure-hunting, the daughter informed she was coming or else . . . and we were off to Riddrie Park Cemetery on the outskirts of Glasgow.

Our mission was to hunt down the grave of the grandparents of an old friend, Helen Sinclair, who is staying with us for a few days. She was brought up in New Zealand and now lives in London but is determined to be buried in the country she has always considered, with typically fiery passion, to be her native land. She wants to lie one day in the soil of Riddrie beside the Scottish grandparents she never knew, who died within a tragically short time of each other in 1910 and 1912, leaving four young sons who were then farmed out among relatives around the world.

Helen's father fetched up in New Zealand, where he became a

229

sheep farmer, married the beautiful descendant of a Maori princess and taught his daughter that she was a Scot and never to forget it. She didn't. A fervent member of the Free Church of Scotland, she has bought a lair beside her Sinclair grandparents and is looking forward with what can only be described as zest to their future co-habitation and a happy meeting after the Second Coming.

The trouble is, as she told us when we turned into the cemetery, she last visited the grave thirty years ago, couldn't remember the lair number and had only the haziest notion of where her future residence was to be found. A tall, plain stone, she thought, possibly on a corner. We would find it, we vowed.

We fanned out across the cemetery, tramping through the damp leaves and peering at the faded lettering on the oldest-looking stones. There were a lot of corners, we discovered, a lot of tall, grey stones and an awful lot of Sinclairs, none of them the Jane and William who had died in 1910 and 1912.

The shadows lengthened and the leaves stirred and still we searched. I waited for either the most imaginative or the most lazy of the brood to precipitate a stampede back to the car by announcing that the trees looked like witches and the graves were starting to open, but they were all too intent on being the one to beat the others to the right stone.

To be honest, I thought we might be treated to a morbid observation or two on mortality by the second youngest, who has reached the age where the implications of death begin to baffle and worry. He regularly works himself into a state of tearful anxiety before going to sleep about who will look after him if his father and I should die. Your aunt, I say. And what if she dies? Your other aunt. And what if she dies? Your uncle. And if he dies? Some very kind and loving friends. And if they die?

After several minutes of this, he has finally worked himself up to a point where he is entirely alone on the planet, sole survivor of a stray meteor, with no one left in the whole world to kiss him to sleep. The pathos of it all quite overwhelms him.

The last few nights, however, he's been too busy with his teeth. To his inordinate joy and pride, he has lost one at last. 'Actually, I haven't lost it,' he explains carefully to enquiring relatives. 'It just came out.' So entranced is he by the sight of this tiny, perfect, shiny thing – kindly returned after a special plea to the Tooth Fairy – that he has taken to brushing it lovingly every night along with his remaining mouthful. A bizarre sight. In bed he's got much too much to do testing out all the others for wobble potential to concern himself with the end of the world.

The grassy graves held no horrors for him or any of the others this dreich November afternoon. The five of them charged blithely round the cemetery, all gripped by the single-minded and passionate desire to be first to find that elusive stone. Being first is important when you only have a one in four, and increasingly often one in five, chance of ever making it. The competition is cut-throat. Even the dubious honour of claiming first sight of a mouldering old gravestone becomes a matter of the fiercest rivalry.

Helen directed operations from the front seat of the car, where she sat nursing a gammy leg and her pet chihuahua, murmuring from time to time, 'Yes, I do believe that corner looks familiar. No, I might be wrong. These stones don't look quite tall enough. Perhaps if you just try over there . . .'

Had she been able to leave the car and scour the cemetery herself, we might still be there. She is an indomitable seventy-something who has let neither ill health nor fragile finances stop her doing whatever she sets her mind on, from raising thousands of pounds for a medical centre in Romania to the only slightly less daunting task of weeding our garden this week, planting a mass of bulbs and replanting them when the dog uprooted the first lot. We caught her outside one night at half past eleven, bronchitis and all, finishing off some potting.

With Helen on the job we would doubtless have spent the evening peering blindly at identical grey stones. But our feet were getting cold and the zeal of my fearless grave-hunters was beginning to flag. Video death and tea were calling. One by one they conceded defeat and slipped back towards the welcoming car headlights.

231

Yes, we gave up before we found the tall Sinclair stone. But we'll be back.

November, 1997

Rising to the Occasion

The sad thing about motherhood, I am beginning to realize, is that however much you do right, whatever your modest successes in the upbringing stakes, all that your children will ever be aware of is how much you can't do.

Sewing. Costume-making. Mathematical problem-solving beyond Primary 6. Car punctures. Bird names. Knowing whether an elephant can run faster than a giraffe. Computers. Tuning the television. Drawing anything more complicated than a four-walled house. Stocking the fridge with the sort of food that any self-respecting chap would wish to offer to his peers for a midnight feast. It's endless, the list of things that this mother cannot do.

And I haven't even got to the grossest inadequacy, the most culpable failure, the one my children find hardest to bear. I refer, of course, to baking. I can't do it, never could, never wanted to, was never taught how (due to a minor deficiency in my own mother, who was so traumatized by putting the icing on my first birthday cake before it went in the oven that she never tried again).

I have negotiated my way nimbly through years of bring-and-buy sales, school fêtes and harvest offerings with the help of a packet of biscuits here, a carload of Monster Munches there and one memorable stab at chocolate crispies. And when the children talked wistfully about so-and-so's mother's strawberry tarts, which are always sold out in minutes, I would retort pathetically, 'Aha, but did so-and-so's mother interview the Prime Minister last week?' knowing only too well that they would happily forgo any kudos associated with a mother on nodding terms with the Downing Street doorman for one perfectly formed cheese scone.

This is a strategy which I realize I have copied from my own mother who, when it was drawn to her attention that the mothers of other girls in my sister's class had come up with the brilliant idea of sewing on buttons with thread the same colour as their cardigans, would reply, 'Yes, but can their mothers play "The Arrival of the Queen of Sheba" on the mouthie?' As I recall, it didn't cut much ice then either.

Anyway, all this baking business has now reached crisis point. A few weeks ago the eldest son announced that his class was having a bring-and-buy sale and *only home-baking* was acceptable. What? No Kipling cakes, no tins of marrowfat peas from the back of the cupboard, no packets of shortbread fingers left over from last Christmas? 'No, Mum, you really, really will need to try this time. Please, I've never in my whole life had home-baking to take to school. Give it a try, Mum.'

Poor child. It had obviously been searing his soul all these years and I never realized. He would suffer no more. I zipped round to Tesco's, and was soon discovering the hitherto unvisited pleasure of the baking aisle, lingering long over the competing claims of the self-raising flour brands and smugly turning my back on the seductive charms of those ready-to-use packets that you just need to mix with water and hey presto you've got a Victoria sponge. This was to be the real thing. This would be art.

I got home and immediately chickened out. Our guest Helen Sinclair, star of my last column, had just arrived and it was the work of seconds to get her to offer to do it for me. My son went off to school with a tin-load of fairy cakes under his arm and an air of deep satisfaction. Sold out in seconds, he reported that afternoon. Escaped again, I thought.

But it was not to be. The daughter had been eyeing the ingredients with some interest and announced a few days later that she was intending to raise money for Children in Need by selling some home-baking to her classmates. Could I possibly show her what to do?

I showed her all right. I showed her how to measure out flour with a two-year-old standing on both your feet and his nose in the scales. I showed her how to soften butter by placing it in a plastic bowl and sticking it in a hot oven – and yes, you're right, the bowl did melt, the liquid butter poured all over the oven and my husband came rushing in shouting, 'How can anyone be so stupid? It must be in the genes.' (He doesn't usually talk about his mother-in-law like that, but then he knew the birthday cake story and had just burned his hand on the melted butter.)

Finally, I showed her how to spoon so much cake mixture into the paper cases that we could stand enthralled in front of the glass oven door watching each one rise prettily and then collapse over the sides like a sandcastle into a river of goo.

She was pathetically grateful. 'It doesn't matter what they look like, Mum. They'll taste fine.' I had three myself, for which she charged 30 pence, and I must say they tasted OK. Not remotely worth the time, the effort, the loss of a useful bowl or the strain on the marriage, but OK.

She skipped back from school the next day to announce that all the cakes had been sold and she needed more. Bless me if I didn't go through the whole rigmarole again. But I have my limits. When she pleaded for more the day after that, I sent her off with a box of Kipling's fondant fancies. I rather fear she may have been economical with the truth about this consignment, because a little girl came up to me outside the school yesterday and asked breathlessly if I could bake some more of those lovely cakes with the pink icing. Ah, *those* lovely cakes with the pink icing . . . The daughter and I looked at each other and said nothing.

Bliss was it in that dawn to have your friends begging your mother to bake for them; but to be that mother was very heaven.

November, 1997

235

Coating the Misery

The English girls' school head teacher who spoke recently of her dismay that some of her pupils were transported to and from school so indulgently these days that they didn't even possess a coat may have missed an even more insidious development on the mackintosh-front.

I refer, of course, to the refusal to wear a coat. Full-stop. I mean, what do you do when a child would rather face the full bracing hazards of the weather in his blazer than be seen dead or alive with a coat on top of it, who would much rather arrive home sodden than dream of reaching into his bag for the kagoul his mother so irritatingly smuggles in every morning?

The blazer he graduated into after primary school a mere three months or so ago is now a misshapen, shrunken rag; it looks as if it's done a stint on K2. He would no more think of covering it up in the rain or snow than of bending the cheek to a maternal kiss in public or wearing the natty Marks & Spencer thermal vest I bought him last month. It just isn't done.

His younger siblings are no better. Sure, they wear coats, but it is entirely infra dig to zip them up, or, heaven forfend, to think of raising the hood in the rain. You see them in a knot in the play-ground waiting for the bell to ring in the morning, drizzle seeping down their necks, coats flapping open in the wind. As each one straggles in, you observe hoods being surreptitiously pushed down, hats that have been lovingly tucked over ears by persuasive mothers hastily screwed into pockets.

I can only stand there in my thermal head-sock, three jumpers, anorak, trousers and boots, looking as if that assault on K2 were indeed imminent, and wonder. Can it really be that they don't notice the rain and feel the cold?

There are some lucky people, I know, who genuinely don't. Take the piano teacher, who as the icy blasts whistled up her flowery frock last week mused that it was getting on for the time of year when she might have to start wearing tights. I looked in awe from my thickly trousered pins to her bare legs. Not a goose-pimple in sight. You can't even comfort yourself with the thought that she's well padded with something else, because she isn't. She's got a great figure and there is always plenty of it to see, because amid winds, snow and rain her cleavage remains on generous display throughout the year.

Me, I'm cold. I'm always cold. Even on a hot day I'm so convinced it'll turn cloudy later that I cannot be parted from a large bag of woollies, just in case. Sartorial decisions in winter turn on how many sweaters I can get on and still make it into my jacket.

This makes for some tricky decisions when you're invited to the sort of occasion where a high degree of skimpiness is required. Do you go for the wispy number that will make you feel stunningly sexy for about five minutes and then have to spend the evening hugging a radiator? Or do you cover yourself neck to knee in something a good deal less than frothy, and then watch others frolicking about wispily and feel like their grandmother?

There are some occasions, though, just a few, when you get it right, when you watch others shivering and clutching radiators and rubbing hands and you glide around in your unsuitable long-sleeved dress thinking smugly that you would doubtless have succumbed to hypothermia this time if you hadn't played it safe.

Such an occasion was the BAFTA Scotland awards ceremony last week, when it was clear from the moment you stepped into the Scottish Television studios to be welcomed by a force ten gale and a line of lightly clad girls smiling bravely through chattering teeth that this was going to be a cold night out.

There were other clues. Like the way people held on to their coats, weeping, as the cloakroom attendants tried to remove them. Or the way they sat down at the tables and began rubbing their hands in a bracing manner, as if preparing to watch a football match. You half expected someone to get the flask out.

There were cold shoulders and icy breasts. There were all these men dressed in kilts who plainly wished they hadn't. In the end, the best thing about winning an award was being able to escape back-stage into a warmly carpeted room where you could linger awhile in the heat of the photographer's lights and get the circulation back into your feet.

But we're a brave race, the British. Not a bare shoulder drooped or a bekilted knee quivered. We smiled and clapped and cheered and quietly froze, and who would have known? Clearly it's the early training in the primary school playgrounds that does it.

December, 1997

Water Woes

I don't suppose it would be entirely fair to blame West of Scotland Water for the sure-fire precision with which the two-year-old threw up over the twelve-year-old's birthday cake. But that must have been about the only one of the domestic strains of the last week or so that can't be laid squarely at the door of Scotland's least popular water company.

Not that I'm complaining about diesel in the water, you understand. Ours was fine. But I still charge West of Scotland Water with responsibility for the savage butchery of one rabbit followed by prolonged emotional trauma among several children, the nervous breakdown of one au pair, and the even-later-than-usual departure of our Christmas cards due to the fact that I haven't had a chance to write them.

I further charge them with the stress that is about to be occasioned to my father when he opens his Christmas present and finds he has to wax enthusiastic about a £1.99 book called *Not Won the Lottery Yet Then?* because I missed out on the week it usually takes me to find anything interesting for him. Lastly, I charge them with general responsibility for the premature unstitching of those few precious shreds of sanity that might otherwise have held together until Boxing Day.

Why? Because the school was closed. Suddenly, overnight, in families all over north-west Glasgow, the delicate balancing act we're all practising at this time of year between work and school and shopping and posting and general dashing about was toppled. Mothers who had been reckless enough to plan a working day on the wild assumption that their children would be safely at school were left high and dry.

That first day I set off from home at 7 a.m. to interview a priest on a submarine (as one does), leaving the children to be dropped off at school by their dad on his way to work. At 11 o'clock, en route to the next interview, I phoned home to check that all was well with the au pair, whom I had left planning an undemanding day of paints and puddles with the two-year-old.

The phone was answered instead by a sobbing son whom I had imagined to be well stuck into decimals at the time. He couldn't speak for crying. 'Why are you at home?' I asked. He couldn't answer. He must be ill, injured, meningitis, broken leg, expelled for kicking a football through the head's window. 'What's wrong with you?' I yelled.

'She's killed it.'

'Who's killed what?'

'The dog . . . sob, gasp . . . she's killed a rabbit. We took her out to play and she caught this rabbit and it was screaming and screaming and she wouldn't let go . . . howl, gulp . . . and she's still got it.'

His sister then grabbed the phone to sob that she'd been bitten when she tried to rescue the rabbit and was severely injured. A younger brother pushed her out of the way to inform me that she was exaggerating her injuries and he was pretty sure the rabbit had got away but he hated the dog and why wasn't I there?

At last our Czech au pair made it on to the line to report that their father had found the primary school closed, deposited them all back home and then disappeared. A rabbit had indeed been savaged by the dog, all four of the children currently on her hands were crying but the bite was not serious, someone had arrived to deliver the .new freezer, where should she put it and what should she do for lunch? If her English had been up to it, she might have added that this was not in her job description. She sounded frazzled.

Should I go home? Thoughts of Louise Woodward fought with images of the film crew waiting for me, the endless trouble it would cause to pull out now. I wondered if the education authority had weighed up the problems of operating a school without water with the risks of inadequate childcare for those suddenly forced to stay at home. I stayed with the job. When I finally got home, the au pair collapsed into bed with nervous exhaustion.

The next working day I managed to place the children in assorted friends' houses. I collected them all later and raced back to prepare a birthday tea for the eldest who, in what he considered a bitter irony, was the only one still at school. That was when his youngest brother saw fit to vomit over the cake.

I had earmarked the next day at home for cards, present-buying and putting the tree up. Instead I paid back my childcare debts and had seven children swinging from the lampshades. And so the week went on. The cards never got written, the shopping trips were never made, the working days were a nightmare of last-minute organization, and the children had a ball.

Mind you, I wouldn't want it to be thought that I'm not counting my blessings. At least I could bath them *en masse* at the end of the day and mop up the copious rivers of vomit with clean tap water, unlike the friend whose child chose that week to start bed-wetting. She quickly had her fill of handwashing duvets in mineral water, and decided to stick with the washing machine. Sheets, clothes and house are still reeking of diesel.

In fact, she tells me she has been talking to a number of others whose children unaccountably started wetting the bed just at the very moment when their mothers would find it most difficult to cope. This, she reckoned, was a sinister development.

Mass bed-wetting in north-west Glasgow – another charge to lay at the door of West of Scotland Water? I trust the enquiry will look into it.

December, 1997

The Christmas Salmon

I would love to say that our festive season will be remembered for the many unprecedented tributes to my roast turkey and the look on my sister's face when she opened an enormous crate of a present from her six-year-old nephew and found it to contain two Opal Fruits.

These touching thoughts may indeed surface from time to time in the future. But I suspect the real memories of Christmas 1997 *chez nous* will be a good deal less sentimental.

Boxing Day was when the rot really set in. Sisters, brother and I took a gaggle of children to the funfair in Glasgow's SECC, the place you visit out of sheer masochism at this time of year to have it proved to you beyond a shadow of self-delusion that you are no longer young. You can act youthful and feel youthful, but unless you can sit on that evil Waltzer looking studiedly bored while some sadistic eighteen-year-old spins you like a top, you've got to face the facts: you're past it.

I staggered home feeling ill, to be met at the door by a sheepish-looking husband and the powerful stench of overdone salmon. The man behind the counter at Tesco's, it transpired, had advised him to poach it in the dishwasher. 'The dishwasher?' I squeaked, being – like him – not too hot on the ways of the culinary avant-garde. He assured me that he too had expressed considerable incredulity, but that two other people in the fish queue had chipped in to say that, of course, that was how you poached a whole salmon. In the dishwasher. Hot cycle.

So he had dutifully emptied the dishwasher, placed this whacking great fish on the bottom rack, whipped the dial to the heaviest duty setting, switched on and left it to get on with the job. While I was tottering on and off the rides at the SECC, thanking my lucky stars that I had gone easy on lunch but blissfully unaware of the fate of my supper, he was stretched out on the bed reading a book. And down below a boiling salmon was splattering its last.

The problem, as my brother-in-law was quick to point out next day when he came over to help suck fish gunge out of the stricken machine, was simple. When poaching a salmon, one covers it with foil. This was clearly a point deemed too blindingly obvious for the man at Tesco's and the people in the fish queue to mention. But nothing is too blindingly obvious when it comes to cooking in our house, no level of stupidity too lofty for anyone offering helpful tips to take into consideration, and I'm wondering if we have grounds for compensation.

Because, you see, when we had removed the stinking fish and tried to clean the dishwasher, we found the machine wouldn't stop making the most awful, protesting whine, even when it was switched off, and we couldn't disconnect the electrical supply, because the chap who fitted our new kitchen had helpfully fitted the socket behind the sink cupboard. So we had to go to the fuse-box and plunge the kitchen into darkness in order to get the noise stopped. By morning, all the milk had gone off in the fridge, the noise started up again as soon as we put the mains switch back on and the odour of blasted salmon still hung in the air.

But there's nothing like the smell from a dog who's been suffering all night from an upset stomach to put fish pong into perspective. 'What on earth did you give her to eat last night?' I asked as we abandoned the unstoppably whirring dishwasher to follow the trail of excrement upstairs and into the guest bedroom, where she had tried out various positions on the avocado carpet. My husband looked sheepish again. 'Salmon,' he murmured. 'Lots of it.'

While he and my brother-in-law stuck plungers down the dishwasher, I did the needful on my hands and knees with a bottle of Dettol. My sister was meanwhile whisking round the house with the vacuum cleaner. She reckoned the housework was getting me down, and so it was. Ever since our alarm went off by accident when we were out one day before Christmas and two burly members of Strathclyde constabulary were kind enough to investigate, I have been a little defensive about domestic tidiness.

They found the back door wide open, you see. It was, of course, our multi-talented dog who had opened it, and anyone who would like to relieve us of this beast as a small kindness should submit their bid in a sealed envelope. But the officers were not to know that, and their excitement mounted as they crept through the house and found drawers hanging open, cupboards with contents spilling everywhere, possessions scattered far and wide, cushions on the floor and every sign that an ace team of burglars were about to be caught in the act.

By the time I got back, the police had found my husband's number, phoned him up and been assured that their description sounded just the way our house always looked. At his invitation they had made themselves a cup of coffee in the kitchen while keeping the dog at bay and lamenting the crime-bust that never was.

It was all very embarrassing, and just as my grandmother used to feel passionately about always having clean underwear in case she got whipped into hospital unexpectedly, I plan to urge any grandchildren of mine to keep their houses tidy at all times because you never know when you'll come home to find two charming police officers sipping coffee in your kitchen.

I will also be warning them that it is always a good idea to remember the tin foil when you're poaching salmon and to watch what you feed the dog if you're daft enough to own one. Otherwise, I'll be sure to say, Grandma may have to tell you all over again what happened that Christmas of 1997.

January, 1998

PART FOUR

Cow'rin' Beasties

Among the many Scottish verses to which our house resounds at this time of year in honour of Burns Night, we are currently enjoying moving tales about a hoggie, a laverock and the Loch Ness monster. But no mice, thank goodness. I lived in dread of 'To a Mouse' appearing on the agenda again, because it's just not politic to dwell too fondly on images of wee, sleekit, cow'rin', tim'rous beasties with panic in their breasties, when you're in the process of exterminating them.

'Oh no, not the mice. Surely you're not going to write about the mice,' groaned my mother in tones of deepest mortification. There are some domestic barrels, she intimated, that ought not to be scraped. Mice are like head lice, she reckoned: we may know they are no respecters of cleanliness and gentility, but it's still not the sort of thing you mention in polite company and newspaper columns. Still, she's nipped off out of the country on holiday, so she'll never know.

Now I have nothing against mice in person, as it were. I could tolerate a whole tribe of them as soon as look at one spider. But I'm not wildly enthusiastic about their droppings. When I discovered the little black calling cards not only behind the fridge and in the pan cupboard, but inside a bed amid traces of the daughter's midnight feast, I announced that these mice had to go. I was calling in the pest control man forthwith.

Howls of protest greeted the news. How could I be so cruel?

(this from the second son, who's a soft-hearted 'To a Mouse' sort of chap). They weren't doing any harm (this from the daughter who didn't have to clean the muck out of her bed). You've got to expect mice in a farmhouse (from the husband whose contribution to general levels of cleanliness in the house is equally negligible). Let's get a cat (from the eldest son who appears to have forgotten what the dog has already done to the rabbit and the gerbil).

I must say I held my own pretty well against this onslaught. The motion was grudgingly carried in the end when I asked how they would like it if the two-year-old sprinkled his ice-cream with mouse-droppings.

The pest control man from the council arrived next day and went round the house placing little trays of what looked like wheat husks in all the places the mice had appeared. He talked about his victims rather tenderly, as if this were indeed ambrosia he was being kind enough to prepare for them.

'Ah yes, they'll like this. They'll be out tonight for a good tuck-in, bless them.'

'What does it do to them?' I asked, mindful of my baleful family.

'Oh, it goes for the nerves,' he said cheerfully. 'Doesn't take long. I'll come back in a week or two and we'll see if they've enjoyed it.'

Two days later the eldest son opened the dog's feed packet and found, curled inside, a dead mouse. The whole family clustered round, gaping at the small hole chewed in the packet and the tiny creature lying inside on top of the Winalot wholemeal mixer, which it had undoubtedly noticed was full of crunchy goodness. It looked just like our dear departed gerbil before it was eaten last year by the dog.

Six pairs of eyes glared accusingly at me. 'Well, it looks quite peaceful,' I said defensively.

There were other signs of successful extermination. The droppings had stopped appearing and the dog, her digestive system still a mite delicate from the ravages of the Christmas salmon, produced some more dramatic messes on the floor, which my husband claimed was obviously because she had been eating dead mice and was being slowly poisoned. He suggested this was a machiavellian plot of mine to get rid of mice and dog in one fell swoop.

I said this was nonsense and she was equally obviously still suffering the ill effects of the salmon which, you may remember, he had in an excess of enthusiasm for nouvelle cuisine, consigned to the dishwasher for some considerable time without foil.

However, I have to admit that my friend the pest control man did say it was quite possible that the dog had been eating dead mice. He explained with some relish that there is something in the poison that makes the poor mites claustrophobic. This was apparently developed after complaints that mice were expiring behind fridges and cookers and leaving an awful smell; now the mixture had been modified to make them rush for space before dying. I decided to keep quiet about these findings.

On his return the mouse man went round the house inspecting all his little trays and exclaiming with pleasure at finding them disturbed.

'Oh yes, they've enjoyed this one,' he said genially, carefully removing from one a few bits of fluff, a nail and a block of wood. 'You see, they don't want any other mice to enjoy the food after them, so they try and hide it. It's their secret hoard. My oh my, just look at this one.'

He had pulled the board out from under the fridge to reveal a cairn built from bits of stone and rubble. The tray of goodies was entirely hidden underneath. It was a mouse fortress, a piece of perfect architecture.

The pest control man was so excited that he took a photograph. I was torn between pride at providing such a perfect specimen for the best control archives and sympathy for these creatures working so hard to build their pyramids of detritus to protect the food that was killing them.

Ah well. As Burns could have told them, the best laid schemes o' mice an' men gang aft a-gley.

Just don't tell my mother.

January, 1998

Poggles

Genes are disconcerting things. I've been reading that fine news-paperman Jack Campbell's account of his years at the *Scottish Daily Express*, revelling again in the tales of journalistic derring-do I remember so well from my parents, who both worked there more than forty years ago in what the survivors of that era always refer to mistily as the heyday of Scottish journalism.

At the end of Chapter 18 I was intrigued to see my own name looming up. As Jack describes it, both Magnus Magnusson and his wife Mamie Baird 'were relegated to a subsidiary role as we introduced to the reading public their three-month-old daughter Sally in a picture four columns wide under a banner headline which blazoned the news of Mamie's Baby.'

And that was only the start. Prompted by Jack Campbell's book, I got the parental newspaper files out and discovered that some months later my mother began writing a series of domestic chronicles from home, keeping readers of both the *Express* and Glasgow's *Evening Citizen* fully briefed on the riveting exploits of her first-born.

This innocent child had been saddled with the nickname Poggles, derived from *to poggle*, a verb of unknown family origin meaning to interfere with, spill, mess, get in among and generally be where you shouldn't. Although I'm delighted to report that the name Poggles did not long outlast the column, the verb did and remains to this day an indispensable addition to the family lexicon, as in 'Who's poggled the video recorder?' or 'Someone's been poggling in that fridge again.' The vocabulary of toddlerhood in our house would be much impoverished without it.

'POGGLES IS HERE NEXT WEEK,' announced the *Evening Citizen* breathlessly one Saturday. *'Who is Poggles? You will find out on Monday.'* Come Monday, a photograph of nineteen-month-old Poggles appeared with the caption 'Dimples behind her knees' and an article by Mamie Baird which set the tone for the months to come: 'Believe me, Life With Poggles is a thousand times more hectic than the toughest assignment I ever tackled.'

There followed articles about Poggles and tantrums, Poggles and teeth, Poggles talking to the milkman's horse, Poggles refusing to sleep at night. Under the writer's byline at the top of the piece would be a little explanatory paragraph such as: 'By Mamie Baird – Poggles's mother, until recently a fairly hard-boiled newspaper-woman who thought she could handle pretty well any situation. She is now realising her mistake.'

I trawled through the old, faded cuttings, both entranced and increasingly discomfited. Here was I thinking that my own column here was a model of originality in a style all my own, only to discover that my parents were doing exactly the same thing forty years ago and in a style uncannily similar.

I say 'parents' advisedly, because my father kept getting in on the act as well. Although the cuttings confirm that he spent most of his time on the bread-and-butter journalistic issues of the day, he too was hauled into the soft stuff from time to time. One column bylined 'By *Mr* Mamie Baird' began:

If it's all the same to you lot, I'm having a shot at doing the wife's column this week. She's been having a baby.

This takes up a bit of time, apparently. What with this and that, she claimed that she just hadn't been able to get round to dashing off a few lines on the subject of this baby lark.

Don't blame ME. I offered to bring the typewriter to her very bedside. I showered pens, pencils and paper over the counter-pane.

But no, she said, with a dreamy doe-eyed sort of look at Little Sister lying in her cot sleeping off the last milk-binge, no, she said, there just hasn't been time.

As you can well imagine, I insisted on a pretty detailed excuse – a minute-by-minute account of what she was DOING with all her time. I mean to say, it's the thin end of the wedge, isn't it?

For a couple of summers they joined forces to do an *Express* Family Magnusson on Holiday series, in which they toured Scotland in a small caravan, chronicling the vicissitudes of life on the move with a small child and concluding that they rather wished they hadn't. Their final piece in the series – headlined STAY AT HOME TILL SHE GROWS UP A BIT. By Magnus and Mamie. Somewhere in Ayrshire' – began: 'No, don't do it. That's our considered opinion.'

Much the same view, come to think of it, as I reached in these pages not so long ago. But *Express* readers were a more hardy lot. A spate of letters poured in, challenging this wimpish couple. One began: 'We cannot believe that you consider your experiences either typical or helpful. We fear that numerous young couples have been laughing heartily at you.'

The *Express* immediately launched a competition for the best Holiday with Baby stories and were inundated.

Meanwhile, as the number of babies increased, the *Citizen* column became more and more frenetic. In June 1960 my mother was writing it between contractions, flat on her back on a stretcher on the way into the labour room for the birth of the third baby. Three weeks later they were moving house. It must have been one of the longest flittings in history, because the *Citizen* splashed the account over five consecutive days. On day three Baird was writing: 'The windows are bare. The shelves are empty. There are no carpets on the floors, no cushions on the chairs. And father has gone off with auntie, and left me holding three crying weans – one with wind, one with teeth, and one with sunburn.'

Ah yes. So like the present home life of their own dear

daughter. So very like my own dear column. Is there no escape from the genes?

Still, even if they scupper any pretensions to originality, the parents are always good for a helping hand. Even forty years later, they can help you fill a column.

February, 1998

Time to Go

When I started these articles two and a half years ago, I had a baby. He used to snuggle into my neck and I wondered at the smoothness of his skin, the downy softness of his head. He would gaze at me in a milky stupor and I would gaze back, besotted. He would lie on the bed, gurgling happily, and we would coo and goo at each other till the cows came home. Or at least till his siblings came home from school.

Somewhere, aeons in the future, I could dimly perceive a future when he might conceivably develop a will, a temper and a set of inclinations that might not entirely coincide with my own. But it was hard to believe. He was so mild, so affable, so very delighted to oblige. I grant you it was sometimes a different story at night, but by day he was a joy. Goodness, he even caused a sensation by being the first child in the family to take a nap after lunch.

Cut to yesterday. I finally closed a lengthy negotiation about whether or not he was going to get into that car by hauling him off the ground, yanking the drumming heels in the air, inviting him to stop yelling 'No, No, No' or I'd spank his bottom so hard he wouldn't be able to sit down for a week, and shoving him into his seat with a force that I am rather glad an officer from the RSSPCC was not there to witness. Ah, my baby, where have you gone?

The compliant infant has metamorphosed into a terrible two-year-old with a will of iron and a breathtaking capacity for tantrums at the first hint of thwarted desire. This time last year I was beginning to wonder if he would ever begin to speak. Now he's formidably articulate, with a relentless line in bargaining and a lethally effective ability to fire off a 'Why?' when you're in full authoritarian flow.

At this very moment he is bouncing up and down on my left thigh while I struggle to type at the computer, commanding me to press the sequence of keys that will bring the Millie's Math House programme to the screen. 'Why not, Mummy?' 'Because I'm trying to write a story here.' 'Why, Mummy?' 'Because there's a man waiting for it in an office and he'll be sad if I don't finish it in time.' 'Why, Mummy?' 'Because I've promised to write it for him.' 'Well, I've got a good idea. We'll just play Millie's Math House and you can write to the man later. OK, Mummy?'

No, not OK, I'm afraid. In the end we compromise and in return for his leaving Mummy's story alone and ceasing to press the CAPS LOCK key, I agree to act as his evil sidekick in this week's favourite game.

He returns with a Roman helmet on back to front and a yellow plastic duck. 'Aha!' he thunders, brandishing his weapon. 'I'm a bad guy. You're the other bad guy. Let's go and kill people with this duck.' The benign influence of the Teletubbies, I may say, has yet to penetrate this household.

Most of my column-writing over the last couple of years has been done in this way with one child or another writhing on my knee, hanging off my neck or sitting on the keys; I've never been very good at the closed-door policy. Now I've decided on a revolutionary new notion: this one involves Mummy not attempting to write at all for a while.

I reckon it's time to give the columns a rest and the two-year-old some respite from the demands of a deadline that invariably conflicts with the schedule he's mapped out for the morning – a murderous battle or two, a couple of forays into Millie's Math House, a play shop involving numerous purchases of pounds of mince, maybe followed up by cuddles in front of the *Pingu* video.

Like so many youngest children in a large clan, much of his life is wrapped up in the needs of his siblings. He spends what must seem like an eternity in the car, dropping people off, picking them up and zooming away for a thrilling sojourn at the supermarket.

The compensations, of course, are the endless supply of playmates, access to electronic toys that his eldest brother had to wait nine years to get his hands on and early tuition in the vocabulary needed to make his way in the world. His advanced grasp of phrases like 'It's not fair', 'It wasn't me' and 'Shut up, you fat pig' should stand him in good stead if he ever fancies becoming a Glasgow councillor.

But other benefits, such as individual attention or pursuits of his choice carried out at his pace, are harder to come by in a big family, which I suspect is why he is more prone to tantrums than the rest were. Although we all know that the best way to deal with a tantrum is to pre-empt it by careful distraction long before it gets to the point of no return, this is a strategy that requires time and patience, both of which are in dwindling supply by the time you get to child number five.

Soon he'll be starting playgroup; then it will be a fast course through nursery to school. So these weeks and months with him now are infinitely precious. The baby has gone. The two-year-old, with his wilfulness and his contrariness, his extravagant affection and his glorious imagination, will not be at this stage for much longer either. I want to enjoy it with him.

That's why I'm off now to shoot some good guys with a duck.

February, 1998

EPILOGUE

Big Thoughts

The other night I was compering a rather posh concert. Standing in the wings, awaiting my cue to sweep on to the stage and welcome the audience, I heard myself being introduced. 'Journalist, blah, broadcaster, blah, writer, blah, but most amazingly of all, MOTHER OF FIVE.' I fancied I could hear a collective intake of breath, a low murmur of astonishment rippling round the auditorium. The fulsome announcer might just as well have mentioned that, most amazingly of all, I had recently grown a second head. 'Please welcome her now, our host for the evening, the woman with two heads, I mean five children, Sally Magnusson.'

When I recounted this story later, my husband was not impressed. 'Start to worry when there's no intake of breath,' he said briskly. 'That'll mean you look like a mother of five.'

And what, pray, does a mother of five look like? Plump apple-pie cheeks and flour on her apron, I suppose. A kindly earth-mother. The sort of character who belongs to another time and another place, who somehow missed out on the news that the world has changed and that two children (preferably one of each sex) are what's acceptable these days.

There's no denying that big families are becoming a curiosity. Wherever you go, the message is plain, from the 'family tickets' which invariably include only two children, to hotel room bargains, luxury holiday prizes on the back of Corn Flake packets, restaurant tables and the kind of cars that the Chancellor now wants everyone to buy. A family with three children borders on the socially acceptable, four children is pushing it, five is beyond the pale, six is lunacy and seven can only mean you're a friend of the Pope.

There are perfectly good reasons why families are getting smaller, of course. We all aspire to give our children the best, to dress them nicely, feed them well, give them treats, take them on holiday and fulfil their Christmas fantasies, but it has become a frighteningly demanding business. To take advantage of the opportunities undreamed of by the last generation, to enable your children to enjoy what they see others enjoying, can involve a staggering commitment of resources. It makes sense to limit the numbers and do properly for one or two what you could never contemplate for three, four, or five.

As a matter of fact, this is something I'm only just beginning to realize. Financial planning never figured in our family planning. With the exception of the last conception, where social conscience and financial reality were belatedly beginning to impinge, we never thought about it much at all. Our rather lame excuse for the breathless succession with which baby followed upon baby was always that it seemed a good idea at the time.

And so it was. We have never had a moment's regret. But babies don't cost much; it's only now that we're beginning to understand what others presumably think about from the start; that in the matter of family size, more inevitably means less.

Our tribe have had to learn that families of seven don't jet off to foreign parts at the drop of a school holiday. They have had to understand that one family outing to McDonald's could keep us in groceries for a week. They appreciate that when there are five to be shod for school, a request for the latest designer trainers is not going to get very far. They see the same clothes circulating for years. They know, too, that after-school clubs and exotic sporting activities have to be ruthlessly rationed, because the chauffeur has her limits.

They spend more time at home than many of their peers, because the sort of casual day trips that smaller families take in their stride require feats of organization that their parents are not always up to. The older ones find their aspirations constantly thwarted by having to take into account the conflicting interests of younger ones. Sitting through a film like *Barney the Dinosaur* when your taste runs to *Terminator II* is not an experience our twelve-year-old would recommend to anyone. At home, they may find themselves hauled away from *The Simpsons* to read *The Cat in the Hat* to the three-year-old or denied permission to send away for a Nintendo fighting game deemed unsuitable for the febrile imagination of the six-year-old.

On the other hand, they are a gang. The pleasure they derive from the others' birthdays gives them five a year. Toys and games are effectively pooled and friends shared. They may irritate each other beyond endurance at times, but they're never lonely. Our type of holiday may not, as I'm constantly informed, be worth boasting about in the playground, but at least there's always someone around to bury in the sand.

We like being a big family. Life may be noisy and messy, and I sometimes look enviously at friends who embarked on maternity at the same time as I did but who finished sooner; they now preside over civilized meals and end the night in the same bed as they started. But the bonuses outweigh the disadvantages. I think possibly the greatest bonus of all is that in an age characterized by high expectation and low satisfaction, big families by and large tend to expect less and enjoy more.

Since having a large gang of children discourages many of the headier lifestyle aspirations, you come to relish the smaller pleasures. Something as mundane as a roomful of children quietly doing their own thing, with the youngest practising his hopping and the next youngest reading out his latest story ('And then the pig askApt from the farm') can transfix you with happiness. It's an attitude of mind which at core has nothing whatsoever to do with the size of the family. But big ones certainly foster it.

I was thinking about that this summer, a few months after I stopped writing the columns, when we took a rented caravan and a small tent on a five-day excursion to the North of England. This was not, as the children were quick to point out, Florida, Majorca or the Algarve, and nobody except my husband, who had picked up the tent for £50 at the sales and was dying for a chance to try it out, held out much hope for the holiday at all. But we won't forget it.

The first unexpected gem on our sun-seeking meandering down the A1 was the historic holy isle of Linda's Farm. We never did get to see any relics, since the daughter lost interest when it was explained to her that this was not the place to go for pigs and horses, Linda's or anyone else's, and her six-year-old brother was only interested in finding the sea and being, as he put it, 'squashed by some waves'.

Leaving our driver contemplating how to execute a three-point-turn at the end of a narrow track with a caravan at your back, the children and I clambered over the dunes and set off across a beach as wide as the Sahara Desert to the distant sea. The wind, which we had barely noticed before, was racing across it like a demon, whipping the sand into our eyes and slapping it against our bare legs. Feeling like Lawrence of Arabia, we battled to the water's edge, where some of the children struggled into swimming costumes and hurled themselves into the icy breakers. Most of their clothes were later located under neat piles of sand, but if any future visitor to Lindisfarne should happen upon three socks and a T-shirt, they're ours.

'This is the first sand-storm I've ever been in,' yelled the daughter above the screaming wind, as we stumbled back across the desert. She could not have been more enchanted with a Disney theme park. 'This is great. It's really great.'

Ahead of us, barely visible through the veil of sand, a lone figure could be seen on a far outcrop, waving. Even at this distance, I could tell he was looking smug. And sure enough, there was the caravan waiting for us, pointed triumphantly in the right direction.

We fetched up that night, for reasons that now escape me, in a site just outside the market town of Barnard Castle. I think we imagined ourselves passing the night in the romantic lea of the castle, with battlements overhead and peacocks strutting by at dawn. We didn't realize that caravan sites, wherever situated, are actually just fields filled with, well, caravans.

But even here were unlooked-for pleasures. Hot showers, clean loos, a place to wash the dishes, a whole universe we never knew existed. Bumbling through the gates in the twilight, taking eight goes to get into our space, we suddenly realized we were in a different world: the fifties in a field. Gaudy awnings protruded from the side of caravans, creating living rooms with cheerful lamps and televisions flickering under bristling, 1990s aerials. Tantalizing aromas rose from dinky kitchens. Children chattered on the swings. Cheery men in beige zip-up jackets speculated on the next day's weather as they tipped out the potato peelings into tidy bins.

We caravanning ingenues were oddities in this ordered universe, as we basked in an aroma of unwashed feet and ripe trainers, munched on slices of dry bread and ham, tripped over sleeping bags and stormed for the door because somebody – against express orders – had been productively engaged in the chemical toilet. But it was unexpectedly comforting to come in off the road and be part of this quaint, reassuring environment for a while. I began to appreciate something which had always eluded me about caravanning, which is why on earth people do it. Actually, I'm still not entirely sure why the women do it, because clearing up another meal in such a confined space is something I will cheerfully go to all lengths to avoid for the rest of my life, but the men all seem to relish a kind of wagon-train mentality, bustling around with leads for this and tubes for that, enjoying the sensation of holing up the family for the night and battening down hatches against the wind and the rain.

Over the next few days we breezed, literally, around the northeast of England, snatching bits of treasure here and there from the jaws of threatening rain and a recalcitrant caravan. The children fished off Hartlepool pier near their grandparents' home and rode trams round the inspired Beamish museum ('You mean we're only going to be showed old things that happened a long time ago?' grumbled the six-year-old, acknowledged leader of the family's wimp tendency, as we drew near). They spent a blissful morning rummaging through the toy and trinket shops of Barnard Castle, thrilling to a report from one brother that gold-plated dung beetles with Australian crystals were going for bargain prices. Among the pebbles of Seaham beach they found wave-scrubbed stones that gleamed like rubies and emeralds.

Seaham, a surprise coastal jewel itself between the chemical works of Hartlepool and the lumbering cranes of Sunderland, was where my husband said portentously, 'You know what's good about this holiday?' We were lying side by side on the Seaham sands, sun on our faces, jackets buttoned up to chins against the wind in best British seaside manner, watching all five children hunting contentedly for gemstones at the water's edge. 'We've managed to turn a sow's ear into a sow's purse.'

Right at the end, we even managed silk. Leaving behind a piece of the caravan's roof in a low tunnel at the Metro Centre, an oversight we had some difficulty explaining to the hire firm later, we headed back up the A1 and into the pretty Monks Muir site outside Dunbar. There we unshackled the car and drove off in the magical evening light to the beach at Belhaven Bay where, under a vast sky of pinks and blues, we idled across the damp sands and watched the wildfowl picking at the mudflats left by the retreating tide. We could have stayed all evening, but we were hungry.

At Umberto's cheery Italian restaurant in Dunbar the seven of us sat around two tables pushed together and celebrated the small triumphs of a modest holiday. We were, I remember, almost drunkenly happy.

I looked round the table. There was my skinny first-born with a mountain of lamb chops and spaghetti in front of him. Ravenous as always, he had ordered two dishes together. The sun and wind had sent the freckles on his face into wild overproduction. He was creased with laughter at the antics of his three-year-old brother who, between helping himself to something from everyone else's plate, was showing off with daft phrases he knew would make his siblings laugh. 'Helicopters on my toast,' he was shrieking, giggling helplessly at the wit of it. 'Bells aren't chairs. They're not walls either.'

Across from him, the ten-year-old we call the Broccoli King, his face another mass of freckles, was tucking into a special side order of his favourite vegetable. He was asking what that T-shirt the man at the next table was wearing meant. It was something rude about learning to be a gynaecologist. Everyone looked at the man in fascination. We had a long discussion about what gynaecologists do.

Opposite me was the six-year-old, watching the manic performance of the youngest with his impossibly big blue eyes and gravely inviting me to feel his wobbly tooth. He said he was feeling grown-up tonight and dashed off to the gents himself without an escort.

The daughter, with her voguish red vest and the long blonde hair I'd have killed for at her age, was being as competitive as her position in the middle of four brothers has always made her. Her tooth, she intimated, was much more wobbly than anyone else's. Just feel it. She was pretending to understand the gynaecologist joke, just in case her brothers did.

At the top of the table, fending off the three-year-old's raids on his tagliatelli, my husband had that satisfied 'We won the day' look on his face. He began raving about how we could buy a bigger tent and do it next time without the caravan. We could drive to the Continent. We could conquer the world.

This, I reckoned, was why families were worth it, and the bigger the better: because at the end of the day there is nothing to beat the having and the belonging, the banter round a table, the shared achievement of getting through things together.

Looking back on that evening now, it seems to me that the enchanted time on the sands and in the restaurant was representative of something greater. Maybe I'm being fanciful, but it seems to me that what it symbolized was a whole period in the family life-cycle, one that many families cherish and look back upon as especially precious, one that this book has in some ways encompassed.

It's a time when we are all still in the adventure together, children still willing, parents still with the energy to seize the moment. A time when the eldest child still relishes the jokes of the youngest

271

and the company of his parents. A time when we can all still sleep higgledy-piggledy on top of each other. A time when holiday means family rather than raves in Ibiza. A time, too, when we as parents are still poised at the cusp of the generations, nourished by the one as we nourish the next. A time worth celebrating while we have it.